Preaching
The Miracles

Series II, Cycle B

Dallas A. Brauninger

CSS Publishing Company, Inc.
Lima, Ohio

Scripture quotations are from the *New Revised Standard Version of the Bible*, copyright 1989, by the Division of Christian Education of the National Council of the Churches of Christ in the USA. Used by permission.

Library of Congress Cataloging-in-Publication Data

Brauninger, Dallas A., 1943-
   Preaching the miracles : Cycle B / Dallas A. Brauninger.
     p.   cm.
   ISBN 0-7880-0829-3 (pbk.)
   1. Jesus Christ—Miracles. 2. Bible. N.T. Gospels—Homiletical use. 3. Preaching.
I. Title.
BT366.B72   1992
251—dc20   96-5303
                                                CIP

This book is available in the following formats, listed by ISBN:
0-7880-0829-3 Book
0-7880-0830-7 IBM 3 1/2 computer disk
0-7880-0831-5 Macintosh computer disk
0-7880-0832-3 Sermon Prep

To Bob

Editor's Note Regarding The Lectionary

During the past two decades there has been an attempt to move in the direction of a uniform lectionary among various Protestant denominations.

•Lectionary Uniformity

Preaching on the same scripture lessons every Sunday is a step in the right direction of uniting Christians of many faiths. If we are reading the same scriptures together we may also begin to accomplish other achievements. Our efforts will be strengthened through our unity.

•Christian Unity

Beginning with Advent 1995 The Evangelical Lutheran Church in America will drop its own lectionary schedule and adopt the Revised Common Lectionary.

•ELCA Adopts Revised Common Lectionary

Reflecting this change, resources published by CSS Publishing Company put their major emphasis on the Revised Common Lectionary texts.

Table Of Contents

Introduction   7

Miracle 1   9
The Unclean Spirit
Mark 1:21-28
Epiphany 4

Miracle 2   25
The Healing Of Simon Peter's Mother-In-Law
Mark 1:29-31
Epiphany 5

Miracle 3   39
The Leper Healed
Mark 1:40-45
Epiphany 6

Miracle 4   53
Healing The Paralyzed Man
Mark 2:1-12
Epiphany 7

Miracle 5   69
The Withered Hand
Mark 2:23—3:6
Proper 4, Pentecost 2, Ordinary Time 9

Miracle 6   85
Stilling The Storm
Mark 4:35-41
Proper 7, Pentecost 5, Ordinary Time 12

Miracle 7   97
Two Healings:
The Daughter of Jairus And The Hemorrhaging Woman
Mark 5:21-43
Proper 8, Pentecost 6, Ordinary Time 13

Miracle 8   113
The Deaf-Mute
Mark 7:31-37
Proper 18, Pentecost 16, Ordinary Time 23

Miracle 9   125
The Healing Of Bartimaeus
Mark 10:46-52
Proper 25, Pentecost 23, Ordinary Time 30

Bibliography   141

Introduction

As a personal note, early in my preaching ministry, I admitted to presenting just enough biblical text to spring into a sermon that offered primarily an existential interpretation. I wondered if my congregation were also making the leap. More than likely, they wandered somewhere in the gap between the "back then" and the "now."

From these concerns, the interviews commenced. I began to take congregations back to wander with me as askers and observers in the streets of Jesus' day. I hope that sermons born from these three volumes will offer a bridge of understanding between those who journeyed then and those who journey in today's churches as we ready for the new millennium.

Getting the questions going is germinal to exploring a biblical text and to sermon writing and hearing. While this book offers a read filled with information for the sermon writer to develop, the design of its contents provides more than the ho-hum. It avoids presenting a ready-made cloak of words for a morning sermon. The goal of this book is to invite.

The first section of each chapter presents the text of a miracle story within the lectionary cycle. A synopsis of points of action within each story comprises Section Two, "What's Happening?" By reviewing the action of the story, readers define its movement, the conflict, and the change or resolution. Sources are from the New Revised Standard Version of the Bible and the Revised Common Lectionary.

Section Three, "Connecting Points — Conversations," offers the central material of the chapter. Here the author aims to engage preachers in an imaginary exchange before they give the text the usual preparatory attention. A visit with main characters and an occasional bystander nudges readers toward stepping into their sandals. This design invites both the preacher and the listening congregation to become askers of questions relevant for them. As they become increasingly curious, their own question boxes may begin to expand.

Participants in these talks suspend the barriers of time. Besides talking with an interviewer from today, a character from one miracle might reflect upon another miracle or jump into the present world. Beyond study, a preacher might use these conversations as a direct resource for part of the sermon or as a chancel reading.

Each character has voice. Readers ask, "What speaks? What was the character's voice then and what is it now?" Sermon preparers listen to these voices and consider the silences. As they do, they may find the connecting points that bridge the soul of a character in a miracle story with those of parishioners. Putting words into the mouth of Jesus, however, would stretch the challenge. The author attempts only to respond as Jesus might have, based upon his teachings and example.

Listeners become aware of how God speaks to them through the miracle stories. They may also hear better their own inner voices and understand themselves anew. In connecting the past with the present, readers might explore these additional questions: How do the actions within the retelling of a miracle introduce or illustrate an issue important to Jesus? Where is God in this story? What is God's action here? How do the characters relate to us today? What is this miracle trying to tell us about God? What speaks to you? What was a particular character's voice at the time of the story? How would it speak today? What does this miracle say about your own spiritual depth?

Section Four, "Words," lifts up significant words in each story. In this section, the author has relied heavily on research presented in the four volumes of *The Interpreter's Dictionary of the Bible*.[1] While it is not the intent of this writer to present a scholarly study, hopefully this word study offers more than pabulum.

Section Five, "Gospel Parallels," highlights differences and similarities among parallel stories in the gospels. A bibliography follows the text.

----

1. See George A. Buttrick, Ed., *The Interpreter's Dictionary Of The Bible* 4 Volumes (Nashville: Abingdon Press, 1962).

Miracle 1

The Unclean Spirit

Mark 1:21-28 (Luke 4:31-37; Matthew 7:28-29)

---

1. Text

> They went to Capernaum; and when the sabbath came,
> he entered the synagogue and taught.[21] They were as-
> tounded at his teaching, for he taught them as one having
> authority, and not as the scribes.[22]
>
> Just then there was in their synagogue a man with an
> unclean spirit,[23] and he cried out, "What have you to do
> with us, Jesus of Nazareth? Have you come to destroy
> us? I know who you are, the Holy One of God."[24] But
> Jesus rebuked him, saying, "Be silent, and come out of
> him!"[25] And the unclean spirit, convulsing him and cry-
> ing with a loud voice, came out of him.[26] They were all
> amazed, and they kept on asking one another, "What is
> this? A new teaching — with authority! He commands
> even the unclean spirits, and they obey him."[27] At once
> his fame began to spread throughout the surrounding re-
> gion of Galilee.[28]

2. What's Happening?

This healing story is the first pronouncement story in Cycle B.
The pronouncement formula presents a situation, builds to a climax,
offers a solution and gives a statement of the issue. In the early church,
this format made for easier recall of the story for oral retelling.

While healing on the sabbath is mentioned in this miracle, the
main issue is authority. In another Cycle B miracle for Epiphany

7, healing the paralytic (Miracle 4), Jesus observes rumblings and questions among the scribes (Mark 2:6) and challenges them. The fifth miracle in this series (Proper 4), healing the man with the withered hand, also touches on Jesus' authority. However, its main focus is healing on the sabbath.

First Point Of Action
The first two verses state the synopsis of the story. "They" go to the synagogue at Capernaum, and Jesus teaches on the sabbath. Jesus teaches with authority rather than as a scribe would teach. The result brings amazement from listeners.

Second Point Of Action
A man with an unclean spirit cries out to Jesus in the synagogue. He first questions Jesus' role, then recognizes Jesus as a holy person. The unclean spirit voice within the man addresses Jesus with three statements: First, it asks what Jesus has to do with us. Second, it asks if Jesus has come to destroy them. Third, it shows recognition.

Third Point Of Action
Jesus rebukes the unclean spirit within the man. He commands that the spirit be silent and come out of him. Jesus strongly criticizes the evil spirit within the person.

Fourth Point Of Action
The spirit convulses the man and comes out of him with a loud voice.

Fifth Point Of Action
The people in the synagogue who observe this show amazement. They do not know how to explain this. Jesus' actions and authority amaze them. They talk among themselves about it.

Sixth Point Of Action
Because of their talk, Jesus' fame spreads throughout the region of Galilee.

3. Connecting Points — Conversations

Interviewing The Man With The Unclean Spirit

Asker: People suffering epileptic convulsions look as if they are possessed by something completely beyond their control. Is that what happened to you?

Man: It seized my whole being. It was a stranger invading my body. It had its own voice. The words came out of my mouth. In that sense, they were mine. I would not have spoken them if I were given the choice.

Asker: After certain centers in the brain are damaged by a stroke, some people say things they never would have before the injury. Yet, it is the same person inside. The soul of the person, the essence, remains unchanged. Is that what you mean?

Man: I did not want to claim those words as mine.

Asker: You did not ask Jesus to heal you.

Man: I did in a way because the words came out of my mouth. Sometimes our actions speak for us. They do not keep silent. In that sense I asked for help. However, I was helpless to say, "Jesus, something has gone wrong inside me. It feels as if it were controlling me at its whim." Healed now, I feel like an entirely different person. Now I have hope.

Interviewing The Unclean Spirit

Asker: Bear with me on this one, unclean spirit. It is not my style to think about demons as entities, let alone to talk to them. I do not know exactly who you are or what has taken over the person in this miracle. You are negative. You are destructive. However, thanks to the teachings of this story, I know you are not all-powerful. Evil is hard to put a finger on. I give you more power than you deserve by speaking as if you were a person.

   Unclean spirit, you sounded frightened when you spoke out to Jesus. Were you seriously challenged for the first time by someone with more authority than you? You are silent now. Listen, as I have some things to say to you. First, had you not broken the silence, Jesus might not have known you were there.

Unclean Spirit: Evil brandishes no power by being quiet. It thrives on stirring up trouble.

Asker: You recognized Jesus.

Unclean Spirit: Without a doubt.

Asker: The worst thing that could happen to you would be your destruction. When you challenged Jesus, did you hope he had the authority to make a difference?

Unclean Spirit: How perceptive. Sometimes trouble makes itself known with a combination of fear and defiance. I gain power by destroying. I try hard, but ultimately, I cannot stand up to God's power.

Asker: Recognizing something for what it is can reduce its power. Jesus saw bravado for what it was. I still wonder about your asking Jesus what he had to do with you. You used the collective, "us." Does that mean there are several of "you," negative spirits, running around in some nether land? Perhaps "you" refers to you and the person in whose body you live.

I wonder if you are the personification of that dark side in all of us that we do not want to claim. Wherever evil takes hold, the demon called turmoil or the demon called chaos threatens to take over a life. I see one facet of hope as the possibility that we do not have to become our demons. We do not have to lose our identity. When there is mental illness, is it not hope that encourages mental health workers to persevere?

You said, "I know who you are, the Holy One of God." I hear you addressing Jesus with a defiant, cynical voice rather than one of awe. What does the human ear hear when evil appears to speak? What causes people to change from disbelief to a sense of the holy? Is it out of fashion to acknowledge feeling awe in these days of downplaying authority? That might place the person in a secondary position.

Unclean Spirit: I do enjoy scrambling people. Stop a minute, you question box. You are not giving me a chance to get in a crooked word. My turn. Ask in your world of today, what does Jesus have to do with you? What is the relevance of the Holy One of God in your life? How does God care about you?

Somewhere inside each kid on drugs is someone, something, asking the church, "What have you to do with us, Jesus of Nazareth? Can you make a difference, Jesus?"

Somewhere inside men and women who suffer the demon of abuse from a spouse or an adult child is someone, something, asking, "What have you to do with us, Jesus of Nazareth? Do you still care?"

Asker: These questions you and I have been asking — how do we know if I am asking them or if some evil force within me is asking them? I need to talk to Christ.

Interviewing Jesus
Asker: Jesus, if I am to be a whole person, then must I not also claim my negative aspects? Is the evil part what I do not like about myself? How did evil get inside me?

How simple it would be to get rid of the dark side simply by saying to it, "Be quiet." We must have the strength to speak to what threatens to drown us. If God wishes well for us, Jesus, then why does evil exist? Why does God not just keep us all well?
Jesus: I would not snatch your adventure of pondering these lifetime questions by giving you easy answers. However, these thoughts might help. First, when the people of my day witnessed something negative and puzzling, they often saw an evil spirit at its origin. For instance, possession by a demon was the common person's answer for an epileptic seizure.

Now, let us return to where you stopped trying to reason with an unclean spirit. You spoke about telling our dark side to be quiet. Our Creator saw that the world was good, but God did not say it is perfect. Negative elements present themselves in our lives. Disease is not a part of the divine order of things. God does not send sickness. God wishes well for us. God stands with us as inner

13

strength in suffering. "For surely I know the plans I have for you, says the Lord, plans for your welfare and not for harm, to give you a future with hope" (Jeremiah 29:11).

Asker: Jesus, you and the unclean spirit within the man are the main players of this miracle story. The man is a shell that you never address. Still, you call the spirit "he," as if you were speaking to the man. If you acknowledge that the unclean spirit exists, then not only the man perceives it.

Jesus: I recognize the unholy as well as the holy within the person. The unclean spirit recognizes the holy within me. When we admit the presence of both creative and negative energies, then we can choose the attitude we will take toward them. When I say you must love your neighbor as yourself, most people hear "neighbor" but ignore the "as yourself." With forgiveness, we stop allowing a negative part of us to eat us up. We are free to start over.

Asker: Does it make sense, then, to embrace that part of us that we cannot stand? By forgiving it, we subdue it?

Jesus: One way to avoid letting our negative dimensions gain the upper hand is to see them for what they are. Most of us do not suffer from a serious mental illness. However, to a person suffering from an illness called multiple personalities, each personality does seem real. Each speaks with its own voice. Think of evil as one might a chronic illness that surfaces with acute outbursts.

Asker: Then we must call our demons by name. What about your role in this miracle, Jesus? When something has us within its grip, we are helpless to act or think. Are we too weak to silence and expel this demon ourselves? Must we always give over our demons to a greater power?

Jesus: When something negative dominates our lives, we need an ally to stand with us. That may be a trusted friend who offers encouragement when we cannot find courage for ourselves. Hope for change and the improvement of a person's life is strong in this miracle. What is important here is that the man's turmoil could be quieted. Stilled, it could come out of him; that is, he became well. He got over it. He moved beyond the chaos.

Asker: You gave two commands: "Be silent, and come out of him." Must our demons first be quieted down before they can leave us? The man was a passive observer to the demon that convulsed him. He was completely at its mercy. Is this how certain forms of mental illness act?

Jesus: Adults who have let fear or anxiety consume them, whether as the result of a chemical imbalance or from an overload of pressure, seek someone to address the piece of them that can still listen and respond. If the helper can connect, then the sick person begins to trust that core, best part, and to rebuild a healthy life.

Asker: When we can make decisions, we have a choice between good and evil. What credibility does one with an unclean spirit have? Is that period a time-out from ordinary life? What responsibility does the person whom an evil spirit possesses have? Are murderers able to take responsibility for their actions?

Jesus: The person beneath the disease, the soul of that person, is still valid. A most unsettling word in your English language is "invalid." A chronic condition or disease may cause a person to become an invalid; however, it need not make that person invalid. We invalidate the soul of ourselves or of others if we identify and label only by negative energy.

Asker: You acknowledge a separation between the identity of the person and the negative spirit. Does this encourage us to separate from our essence those illnesses and chronic conditions that invade our bodies? The cancer that compromises the whole body does not have to endanger the integrity of the soul. Still, emotional or spiritual stressors can result in burning out the body. Continued burdens of physical pain can sap the spirit.

Jesus: We are mixtures of creative and destructive dimensions. We are free, metaphorically, to shush the destructive and to cheer the creative forces within us. While I have not used your modern word "integrity," I like it. Integrity is the condition of being held

15

in healthy unity. This basic balance harmonizes mind, body, and spirit.

When one part of an individual is in trouble, the whole person suffers. Sickness or unhealthiness shows itself in many forms. The task of the counselor, physician or healer is to discern the source of the discord that is breaking apart a suffering person, and to nudge the sufferer toward reconciliation.

4. Words

Authority

This miracle is about authority. Authority is closely connected with the power to influence or persuade resulting from knowledge or experience. The authority of Jesus brought a sense of his authenticity. One with authority has dominion: You command, I obey. People who feel the threat of an authority ask, "What gives you the right to command? Why do I feel forced to obey?"

In the Old Testament, authority means a legal right. It takes on further meaning in the New Testament as the power to enable a miracle to happen. Jesus had the authority to overcome the powers of evil. He gave the firm command of authority in quieting and exorcizing demonic spirits.

We must take an attitude toward authority. We either accept its validity or reject it. The words, "But I say to you," lead us to respond, "I am listening" or "So what?" Authority is dynamic rather than static. Persons of recent generations have leaned toward rejecting most external authority figures.

One grants authority to another person or recognizes an accepted source as expert information. Consider the element of freedom or right in authority. Students learn to investigate the credentials of an author before they accept a specific, written text as a legitimate source of information.

Final authority belongs to God. Those who question the authority of Jesus ask who grants Jesus authority, how it is that he claims authority and what makes him expert.

God gave Jesus authority as part of the God-person connection. Psalm 111:2-4 suggests the importance of Jesus' works in establishing his authority. "Great are the works of the Lord, studied by all who delight in them. Full of honor and majesty is his work, and his righteousness endures forever. He has gained renown by his wonderful deeds; the Lord is gracious and merciful." (See lectionary Psalm 111 for Epiphany 4 in Cycle B.)

Jesus both recognized his authority and claimed it. Otherwise, he would have had no power to cause change or to perform miracles of healing or exorcism. Jesus accepted his authority as subordinate to God. He was accountable to God. He was in divine partnership with his Creator.

Similarly, those new in their professions, such as seminary graduates, medical interns or maintenance supervisors, must claim authority and believe in their capacity to work in that position. If they can, their attitude is contagious. Their work is effective when they elicit the trust of parishioners, patients or workers. Part of claiming authority or accepting responsibility for our actions involves recognizing to whom we are accountable.

To continue God's acting in the world, Christ entrusted to his followers his own authority to heal and proclaim the coming of the kingdom. Hear the gift of Jesus' authority within the context of the Isaiah hope:

> *For a child has been born for us, a son given to us; authority rests upon his shoulders; and he is named Wonderful Counselor, Mighty God, Everlasting Father, Prince of Peace. His authority shall grow continually, and there shall be endless peace for the throne of David and his kingdom. He will establish and uphold it with justice and with righteousness from this time onward and forevermore (Isaiah 9:6-7).*

Today, electronic authorities tease us. Just because the computer says something does not make it right. We must consider the source. Particularly in election years, voters become leery of candidates who seize television authority. Naivete was spent on earlier exposure to empty voices. Such exposure undermines trust. How do we come to accept anyone or anything as authority once we have become clogged with cynicism? How do we move beyond

17

wariness to listen with a more discerning ear to what a candidate offers?

We are in times of accepting few authorities. How do we measure, size up, an authority? Has the highest American authority become fear of a gun? How did it happen that we have reduced the value of people to the level of things having no conscience? How do we turn this view of the world around so we again grant to a human being value, power and authority simply because of the God-connection?

What about our authority? What authority does our God-connection give to us? Elements include, first, the responsibility to be the best we can be in all situations. Second, those with authority accept responsibility to remember they are children of God. Finally, we know we are valid and we count.

Demons

Demons are spiritual beings who recognized Jesus before followers of Jesus did. A demon, a cosmic power opposed to God, is an unclean spirit. The Synoptic Gospels cite twelve references using the word "demon." In the present miracle story, a separate personality spoke through the individual.

People living in Old Testament days believed evil spirits were the bearers of disease and mental problems. They believed evil spirits took possession of a person. They attributed insanity to the presence of an unclean spirit or a demon. Evidence of suicidal impulses suggested demonic possession. Demonism, or spirit possession, also was a folk designation for epilepsy.

The solution to the problem of demons presented a great difficulty requiring more than physical remedies. Healing came from the spiritual dimension. Jesus regarded disease as one manifestation of evil. A connection lay between casting out demons and recognizing the presence of the kingdom of God. If it is the spirit of God that casts out demons, then the kingdom of God has come. Once these negative spirits were removed, individuals led normal, healthy lives.

Exorcism

Exorcism is the practice of expelling evil spirits from persons or places. Exorcists use incantations and perform certain occult acts. Although exorcism was a common practice then, the Old Testament does not speak of it. According to New Testament writings, Jesus did not use incantations or occult rituals. He met the evil spirits with a stronger, good spirit. Jesus cast out demons by his own words and by the "Spirit of God." (See Matthew 12:28.) Jesus gave his disciples the authority to cast out unclean spirits and to cure diseases and sicknesses. (See Matthew 10:1 and Mark 6:7.) Jesus told them to do this using his name. (See Mark 16:17.)

Miracle

A deepening of faith, is that what a miracle is all about? A beginning definition of a miracle suggests an event that appears unexplainable by the laws of nature. As a result, we say it has a supernatural origin. It is an act of God. It is beyond human power.

Today tempts us to explain away the healing miracles of yesterday's Jesus. The people of that day knew little of what we know now about medicine, we say. In their relative medical and scientific innocence, they only called miraculous what they could not comprehend.

Upon closer look, the healing miracles of Jesus open to us a greater depth of understanding. They pull us beyond the range of certainty into the realm of "maybe." Here we begin to reshape dictionary definitions into a definition of the heart. We see a miracle in Jesus' extraordinary capacity to discern the source of a person's suffering. We recognize a miracle in the creation of the human body and spirit. We find a miracle in human resilience, the capacity to heal, the instinct of the body to respond by healing and being as whole and well as possible.

Willingness to consider a miracle fills us with a mixture of doubt and curiosity. The reality of a miracle awakens us and introduces us to the words and emotions of a less sophisticated time — awe, holy, reverence, admiration. The idea of a miracle invites us to suspend questioning for a moment.

Capernaum

Early in his ministry, Jesus left for Capernaum. Located on the northwest shore of the Sea of Galilee, Capernaum was an important city in the Gospels. Its prosperity was due to the east-west trade route.

Capernaum became the center of Jesus' ministry. He called it his home. He healed many people there; among them were the man with the unclean spirit (Cycle B, Miracle 1), the servant of the centurion (Cycle C, Miracle 7), and the paralytic (Cycle B, Miracle 4).

Unclean And Clean

The idea of unclean has ancient roots in tribal life. To be unclean means to be contaminated by a physical, ritual or moral impurity. Cleanness, then, is the absence of impurities. Unclean could apply to persons, food, places, or objects. This notion evolved into laws administered by priests.

In the New Testament, the demons that cause insanity are regularly called unclean spirits. People believed that only God could bring a clean thing out of unclean conditions. (See Psalm 51:10: "Create in me a clean heart, O God, and put a new and right spirit within me.") This miracle story emphasizes Jesus' gain of authority not only as a teacher but also as one whom the unclean spirits obeyed. Cleansing was part of the redeeming work of Christ as high priest. Sufferers were cleansed by his word. His blood cleanses the whole church. For further discussion about unclean, see Cycle B, Miracle 3.

Sabbath

This exorcism was a sabbath healing. For a discussion of the roles of the sabbath, healing, and Jesus' authority, see Cycle B, Miracle 5.

Scribes

A class of special teachers of the Jewish law, scribes were officials who had charge of legal documents. They served an important role in the foundation of the Jewish religion. As guardians of the Law, they kept close watch on the teaching and actions of Jesus. Their main business was teaching and interpreting the Law, that is, the transmission of traditional legal documents and the preservation of the legal system. These secretaries occupied a special chamber in the royal palace. In pre-Exilic times they held no religious significance.

Scribes and Pharisees were both drawn from the families of the priests, but scribe was a purely secular office. Pharisees, who represented a distinctive class in the community, were a group formed from the scribes. Professional lawyers carried more importance than nonprofessional members of the party. They practiced their legal profession throughout Palestine. The Gospel called Matthew substitutes the elders of the people for the scribes. Given precedence over Pharisees, scribes interrogated Jesus throughout his ministry. See also Miracle 4 and Miracle 5 in Cycle B.

Synagogue

The synagogue, the equivalent of congregation or assembly, was a gathering place used for public worship and instruction. In the New Testament, it appears as a house of worship and a place of assemblage for instruction.

Fear

"The fear of the Lord is the beginning of wisdom" (Psalm 111:10). The word "fear" is not spoken in this miracle story. However, it is present in the questions the unclean spirit asks. Fear involves a wide range of emotions from simple apprehension to dread. In the Old Testament, persons express fear whenever a threat appears against their security and particularly their lives. In the New Testament, fear fixes upon worldly fear, timidity, cowardice, and death. When one's own authority is threatened, as with the power of the unclean spirit, fear is fright. When one accepts the authority of another, fear takes on its positive side, awe.

5. Gospel Parallels

Setting

The collection of words of Jesus that we call the Sermon on the Mount ends with Jesus' words about speaking with authority. Mark and Luke place this miracle in Capernaum (Mark 1:21). As if writing to strangers, Luke emphasizes Capernaum as a city in Galilee (Luke 4:31). While both writers stress Jesus' teaching on the sabbath, Mark places equal weight upon the sabbath and Jesus' teaching in the synagogue. Until verse 33, Luke avoids mentioning that Jesus was teaching in the synagogue.

Response Of The Crowds In The Synagogue

Mark, Luke, and Matthew all report that Jesus' teaching astounded the crowds. Mark emphasizes the "new teaching" and Jesus' teaching with authority (Mark 1:22 and 27). Luke emphasizes Jesus' authority and power (Luke 4:32 and 36). Mark says he taught as one having authority and not as "the" scribes (Mark 1:22). Matthew's two-verse summary emphasizes Jesus' teaching as one having authority and not as "their" scribes (Matthew 7:28). Luke says Jesus spoke with authority but makes no mention of scribes (Luke 4:32).

Following the healing, the response was amazement. Mark reports the crowd "kept asking one another" (Mark 1:27) and Luke that they "kept saying to one another" (Luke 4:36).

Mark's version, with shorter, direct sentences, is more spontaneous than Luke's smoother phrasing. Contrast Mark's "What is this?" (Mark 1:27) with Luke's "What kind of utterance is this?" (Luke 4:36) and Mark's "A new teaching — with authority!" (Mark 1:27) with Luke's "For with authority and power he commands the unclean spirits" (Luke 4:36).

One can hear the amazement in Luke's spontaneous phrasing after Jesus commands the unclean spirits, "and out they come" (Luke 4:36). Mark is staid: "He commands 'even' the unclean spirits and they 'obey' him" (Mark 1:27).

Man With Unclean Spirit

Luke, the physician, is more specific in the diagnosis of the sick man, saying "a man who had the spirit of an unclean demon" (Luke 4:33). Mark is brief: "a man with an unclean spirit" (Mark 1:23).

Both writers say, "he cried out," without defining if it were the demon, the man or the unity (or disunity) of both (Luke 4:33 and Mark 1:24). Luke amplifies, "with a loud voice" (Luke 4:33).

Mark's version, saying "Just then," (verse 23), is more dramatic than Luke's straightforward, "In the synagogue there was…" (verse 33).

Except for Luke's preface with the spirit commanding, "Let us alone" (Luke 4:34), Luke and Mark's three direct statements by the spirit are identical:

"What have you to do with us, Jesus of Nazareth?" Note, first, the use of "us" rather than "me" and, second, the unclean spirit recognizes Jesus and calls him by name.

"Have you come to destroy us?" and "I know who you are, the Holy One of God" (Luke 4:34 and Mark 1:24).

Responding to Jesus' rebuke, Mark reports the unclean spirit convulses the man. Then the unclean spirit cries out with a loud voice and comes out of the man (Mark 1:26). Luke reports the demon comes out of the man after having thrown him down and that the demon did not harm the man (Luke 4:35).

Jesus' Action

The double command of Mark 1:25 and Luke 4:35 for the unclean spirit to be silent and to come out of the man is the same in both narratives.

Outcome

Mark 1:28 stresses the immediate outcome as "At once" and as Jesus' "fame." Less dramatic, Luke 4:37 says, "And a report about him." Mark says "throughout the surrounding region of Galilee" and Luke says "began to reach every place in the region." Luke already told the region in the first sentence of the story, but Mark now identifies the region as Galilee.

23

Epiphany 5

Miracle 2

The Healing Of Simon Peter's Mother-In-Law

Mark 1:29-31 (Matthew 8:14-15; Luke 4:38-39)

1. Text

> As soon as they left the synagogue, they entered the
> house of Simon and Andrew, with James and John.[29] Now
> Simon's mother-in-law was in bed with a fever, and they
> told him about her at once.[30] He came and took her by the
> hand and lifted her up. Then the fever left her, and she
> began to serve them.[31]

2. What's Happening?

The Gospel called Mark wants to set a tone of direct action and
quick response in this story. Mark shows an absence of dragging
feet and suggests a sense of urgency. Jesus gets things done. From
Mark's perspective, whatever happens around Jesus, the response
is always immediate.

"Immediately" is a favorite action word in the first chapter of
Mark. After the baptism of Jesus, the Spirit immediately drives
him out into the wilderness (Mark 1:12). When Jesus calls Simon
and Andrew to be disciples, they immediately leave their nets to
follow him (verse 18). Going a little farther, Jesus sees James and
John. He immediately calls them (verse 20). When Jesus touches
the leper and repeats the healing formula, immediately the leprosy
leaves the sufferer (verse 42).

In the present story of positive expectations, as soon as Jesus
and the disciples leave the synagogue, they enter the house of Simon
and Andrew (verse 29). The disciples immediately tell Jesus about

Simon's mother-in-law (verse 30). The woman's response is immediate (verse 31).

First Point Of Action
With James and John, Jesus leaves the synagogue and enters Simon and Andrew's house.

Second Point Of Action
There they find Simon's mother-in-law sick in bed. They immediately tell Jesus about her.

Third Point Of Action
Jesus comes, takes her by the hand and lifts her up.

Fourth Point Of Action
The fever leaves the woman.

Fifth Point Of Action
As if nothing extraordinary had happened, Simon's mother-in-law begins to wait on them as a host.

3. Connecting Points — Conversations

Mark, in character, tells this story without delays in four direct and compact verses. Because talk is absent in this summary story, readers must fill the pieces. Time stands out as an important element. As soon as they left the synagogue, they went to Simon and Andrew's house (Mark 1:29). We do not know when the brothers became aware of their mother-in-law's illness. However, at the first available moment, they told Jesus about it (Mark 1:30). Jesus acted directly. The fever left the woman. She returned to her duties as homemaker. She was not even the mother of the head of the house. Although she held mother-in-law status, both Jesus and her family recognized her worth.

Unless she claims worth for herself, the aging American woman also holds little value in our society — except possibly for her purse. Today, as in earlier times, a woman has little time to be sick. Typically, she ignores her own needs unless she is doggedly intentional about meeting them. The same call for efficiency by the householder to keep household rhythms in balance, as shown by Simon Peter's mother-in-law, still rings today. If sickness disrupts the rhythm of a woman's role as juggler, everything tumbles to the floor.

Interviewing Jesus

Asker: Jesus, the writers report that you also were silent in this quiet story. Is this because those close to you surrounded you? This is a clean story with no strings attached to the healing. You did not need to prove yourself or make a point. You were at home. You simply did the healing miracle because the relative of a friend had a fever that put her to bed.

Jesus: We often ignore or neglect the common person. We take laborers for granted until their inability to or choice not to work becomes an inconvenience for us. Unconditional love includes everyone. Unconditional love says you and I count.

When I am bone weary and come home to this refuge, this house of my friends and disciples, Peter and Andrew, I often return to Isaiah's words: "But those who wait for the Lord shall renew their strength, they shall mount up with wings like eagles, they shall run and not be weary, they shall walk and not faint" (Isaiah 40:31).

I remember that the one who sustains me does not faint or grow weary. God's understanding is unsearchable. From the sparrows to the very hairs on our head, God numbers us and calls us all by name. So mostly, when I meet a suffering person, these words sound in my heart: "He gives power to the faint, and strengthens the powerless" (Isaiah 40:29). (For further study, read the entire Old Testament pericope for Epiphany 5, Isaiah 40:21-31.)

It is my task and it is your task to remember whose we are and to respond to God's love by caring that much about our neighbor, whatever age, sexual preference, or condition of body and mind.

Asker: In this story, actions speak louder than words. The only report of words was that the disciples did not waste time letting you know Simon's mother-in-law was sick. The first free moment

— at once, the writer said — they told you about her. Your disciples trusted you would take care of things. Was this because of the depth of your friendship?

You responded like the trusted physician whom we give the power to take one look at a problem and know immediately what to do. The disciples did not have to waste your energy with words or long explanations.

Jesus: One dimension of the silence is our familial ease together. It is similar to the comfortable silences between a long-married couple. To reach that level of communication requires the work and practice of trusting. Beyond that, as we become adept at listening with our whole self, we can learn much about another person. The expression on the face of Peter's mother-in-law spoke. The change from her ordinary habits also told me as much as my disciples' focus of attention toward her.

Another element involves the significance of the support of human relationship in restoring or maintaining health. Look at the longstanding sewing or quilters' groups in the rural churches of your day. Do not be fooled into thinking they exist only to make quilts! Your modern-day urban carpool also extends all sorts of supportive possibilities.

Knowing that people care deeply about us and trust we also care about what is happening in their lives helps raise the quality of our living. Isolation can lead to an increased vulnerability to disease and to a shorter life span. Support of others contributes to disease resistance. Opportunity to let off steam among trusted friends is a valuable tool for health. The sick woman was in the right place. The house of Simon and Andrew is probably the most supportive, health-restoring home around.

Asker: Goals and ideals aside, Jesus, when it comes to the whole health of a person, perhaps we should temper your words, "Be perfect" (Matthew 5:48), with these words: Given reality, be in your best possible state of health.

Jesus: Perhaps we should. To be perfect is a goal for our relationships. It is not a command for the condition of the body, over which we have incomplete control.

Asker: Jesus, what do you mean for this miracle to tell us about God?

Jesus: Members of families can give support to each other. In addition, God cares for the seemingly least significant people. Our Sustainer is so aware of us and close to us that very little passes by God. Events of the world, events of nature, and life accidents may pound us down. God comes as a spirit extending a handhold we can depend upon.

God is both approachable and approaches us. That is, God takes the initiative just as I modeled by taking the woman by her hand. Without additional fanfare, without words, God has a way of taking us by the hand. This may be quietness or an inner calm that comes to you in the midst of agitation. It may be the absence of isolation or loneliness when you are alone. It might be the unexplainable clearing of your head when you have been muddled.

Asker: Anything else?

Jesus: Yes, but I'll let Peter's mother-in-law speak for herself about the role we are to play in healing.

Interviewing Simon's Mother-in-law

Asker: You, also, never said a word in this story, or at least it was not reported. Why? Were you embarrassed about being found ill? Did you not know how to respond? Did surprise leave you speechless? Was your faith so automatic and true that you simply accepted the healing as if Jesus had greeted you? Were the words of women in your day considered unworthy? Even so, Jesus thought you counted enough that he healed you. It did not matter to him if you were a man or a woman. Does that not say something important?

Mother-in-law: I suppose my silence could be interpreted as submissive. On the other hand, we were a close, supportive family. I consider Jesus as family. He was at the house often enough. My expectations for recovery were high. Have you not immediately felt better when someone you knew would help came through the door? Jesus is perceptive. He almost can tell what is happening with a look.

The Psalmist says God's job description includes gathering the outcasts of Israel, healing the brokenhearted and binding up their wounds. God lifts up the downtrodden and casts the wicked to the ground. So it is with Jesus. His understanding is beyond measure. So it is with my savior. (See today's pericope, Psalm 147:1-11.)

Asker: You were sick in bed with a fever. You must have been quite ill to go to bed because the woman had to work all day to keep the household going. This role must have been foremost on your mind. The first thing you did upon rising was to get back to your work, your duty, of serving those who had come into the household.

Mother-in-law: You speak accurately about my household duties, but my returning to work was more than duty. Whenever we are freed from what ails us, our first instinct is to return to doing whatever we love most. This is the freedom of health. I guess I would also say it is honoring God's creation of us, of the holy within us. You may also see my actions as a directive, that is, we should put an illness behind us as soon as possible.

Asker: I live in a different age. What are you trying to tell me about what is most basic for me as a woman? For me as part of a family? My family mostly has to take what is left over — not just in meals but of my energy, my emotion, and my love. Was your rising from the bed so automatic that you did not give a second thought to resting a bit? Were you embarrassed again for falling down on the job?

Mother-in-law: What women do share in Jesus' time and in the new millennium is the call to define and redefine who we are, whose we are, that is, that God has made us, and what God calls us to be. I use the word redefine because society continues to evolve. Life brings many accidents and other changes. I would challenge women of your time to study both the negative and the positive connotations of service and being servants. Explore the simple, obvious ways we fulfill what God means for us to be.

Asker: What was it like when Jesus came over to the bed and took you by the hand and raised you up, and you felt the fever leave? You gave the best response of gratitude by immediately returning to your life work.

Mother-in-law: When you are the recipient of the healing touch, the best response is through your own action. My feeling was of deep, unspoken love. It speaks of the closeness coming from familiarity, from family. Jesus did not enter our home, kick off his sandals and say, "Leave me alone, I'm off duty. I'm all done working for today." His directive was kindness and immediate attention toward the members of the family.

Keep the needs of those closest to you in the urgent category. At times, family members use the words or the actions of busyness as a camouflage for their suffering. Extend a symbolic or literal hand.

Interviewing The Disciples

Asker: James, John, Simon and Andrew, who does the telling here? It is all in third person narration without dialogue. Somehow, we assume a disciple is telling the story. The storyteller did not say that Simon and Andrew were present, but only that it was their house. We know only that "they" entered the house and that Jesus and some others, probably disciples, entered with James and John (Mark 1:29).

A Disciple: I was there. Any one of us could have told the story. I told it as I did. I spoke briefly and to the point. I spoke as if it were nothing unusual for Jesus to care for us and for members of our family. It is not that I take Jesus or his healing for granted. Jesus' capacity to heal always surprises me. I hold this person in awe. Jesus has shown me that he is not the ordinary healer of my day. Everything that he does points toward God and God's peace toward us.

4. Words

Woman

Society in the Palestine of Jesus' day demanded respect toward one's mother and, by extension, mother-in-law. Disrespect was

31

punished. Jesus treated women as persons, offering to them the same consideration he gave to men.

The main function of women of Jesus' day was as wife and mother. The ideal woman was trained to love her husband and children. In the patriarchal form of family life, wives belonged to men. Husbands could freely divorce their wives. Subordinate to their fathers or husbands, women held inferior status. A daughter was less desirable than a son. A father could sell his daughter for debt or prostitute her.

A grown woman had considerable freedom to act within her status and role of a wife. Despite the barrier of a husband's ruling over his wife, the woman remained a person. She kept her own name and individuality while being called by her husband's name. She shared in the harvest, manufacture and sale of cloth products. Participating in the arts, she preserved ancient forms of dance and song.

Women performed the rituals of mourning for the dead. Women were present at funerals and weddings. In religious life, they participated in the activities of the great festivals and attended religious gatherings. However, they could not serve as priests because of their ritual uncleanliness.

House Of Simon And Andrew

During his days in the city, home for Jesus was at Capernaum. Readers may infer that Simon Peter took care of his mother-in-law. She in turn served as housekeeper and homemaker.

Simon Peter, the first disciple called by Jesus, was also the most prominent disciple. He is Simon, called Peter, not Simon the Cananaean who was also a disciple. He usually acted or spoke for the group of disciples and is named first within the inner circle of Peter, James and John. Peter, at least, was married. He and his brother Andrew were partners in a fishing business on the Sea of Galilee and lived together at Capernaum.

In the Gospels, Andrew's name is generally used with Peter's. He is identified either parenthetically as Peter's brother or in combination with Peter's name. Jesus called Simon Peter and Andrew as the first two disciples. Next, Jesus called James and John. Gospel reference to these four disciples names them in the order of Peter, James, John and Andrew. Such reference might suggest the order of their closeness to Jesus. Only in the Johannine passage discussing the Greeks who approached Philip wanting to see Jesus is Andrew given individual status (John 12:22). Philip told Andrew of the request. Then Andrew went with Philip to tell Jesus.

Healing

Traditionally, healing means the curing or restoring to health of a sick person. All functions work in harmony, but all parts of the body need not be absolutely free of disease to be in a state of positive clinical health. Consider expanding the definition of healing. Healing can also mean being able again to celebrate life with enthusiasm.[1] Then health becomes a condition of optimal well-being under the best circumstances possible.

Lifestyle, how we manage our life, influences our health. We take environmental elements into our bodies by mouth, nostrils and skin. We see and hear. Whether they pollute or nourish body and spirit, these elements make a difference in the balanced posture of the whole person.

Consider how healing relates to taking sabbath. We take sabbath by ceasing physical effort, recreating both mentally and spiritually and making time for God. All assist in giving honor and restoration to the whole body. All dimensions of the body — mental, physical and spiritual — require a periodic rest to avoid a breakdown. The aim is to balance physical vigor with consistent, functional efficiency. One day off in seven helps us to manage our degree of well-being. Building a few minutes or an hour of sabbath into each day encourages a health-giving balance to our lives. While the miracle of the healing of Simon's mother-in-law is one among the sabbath miracles, for a fuller discussion of the role of sabbath and healing see Miracle 5 of this volume.

Jesus And Healing

The approach Jesus took toward healing brought an advance in thought about sickness and disease. Whenever Jesus met sickness, he made every effort to heal, even and especially on the sabbath.

33

He healed everyone, especially the outcast. He gave no support to the Old Testament idea of disease as a punishment sent by God. In his preaching ministry, Jesus told hearers to repent, that is, to change their wrong ways. His healing ministry did not suggest the suffering were guilty of doing anything wrong. Their action was not to repent but to have faith to become well.

In the Old Testament, the faithful considered health a divine gift. They expected good health. The practice of medicine as we know it had not yet developed. So when disease struck, people had only God to look to for aid. They saw sickness as a spiritual matter. They linked it somehow with sin. Jesus carried forward the Old Testament notion that healing involves revitalizing a right relationship between the person and God. One meaning of "redeem" is to return to ownership. Jesus' redemptive ministry returned people fully to themselves by freeing them from their ailments.

Counselor

Counselors offer advice or guidance. While "counselor " is not a word in this miracle, counseling is implicit in the actions of Jesus. This word returns us to the song giving his purpose: "For a child has been born for us, a son given to us; authority rests upon his shoulders; and he is named Wonderful Counselor, Mighty God, Everlasting Father, Prince of Peace" (Isaiah 9:6).

Jesus' approach to health and healing showed that his earthly ministry was closely bound up with human frailty and weakness, whether of body or soul. He offered kindness to the sick and weak. Jesus paid close attention to the mind and spirit of a sufferer. When he related to a suffering person, he looked at the whole person as if he saw disease as an imbalance within the personalty, not only of the body.

Jesus' actions conveyed his understanding of God's purpose for humankind as salvation and human wholeness. Jesus must have been particularly sensitive to the inner conflicts that brought those who needed healing to their present state of "dis-ease." Were they in some way ill at ease with themselves or with others? Jesus was aware of the possible bearing of emotional conflicts on the beginning of a disease. The healing ministry of Jesus was as much to the mind and spirit as to the body. Part of his healing power was his ability to transform casual talking into a time of healing. He could pinpoint the problem and initiate healing. God gifted him with the ability to listen and hear. In the vocabulary of psychology, he was skilled in non-directive counseling. One might ponder if religion and psychology are not essentially two different ways of perceiving similar processes of moving toward health and wholeness with parallel vocabularies and terminologies.

Mediator

Like counselor, "mediator" is not an uttered term in this miracle story. However, Jesus' role and the friendship role we might share with other members of the church family and beyond as mediators are implicit and deserve mention.

How are we mediators for each other? Suffering is evidence of brokenness and the need for someone to stand with us as mediator and guide. Mediation means the establishment and maintenance of a right relationship between two people. Mediation brings people into communion with each other. It supposes some alienation, an absence of communication or some fighting or conflict. It helps in settling what is unsettled and building bridges that span gulfs.

Gulfs grow between a person and God. Gulfs appear as what is unsettled between two persons. They form as internal divisions within an individual. We learn this assumption from studying the miracle stories: The gulfs in our lives are bridgeable. Something in people's hearts encourages us that we can rework broken feelings. The Christian faith is a religion based on this hope. The goal is atonement. Atonement returns us from a predicament of alienation to a state of wholeness or "at-one-ment."

From time to time, we become so bound up with brokenness that we need a mediator. The people of a church can stand with others as mediators. On a calling card representing a church in Albuquerque, New Mexico, is a cross surrounded by several concentric circles and the words, "circles of healing." Members of that congregation understood they could carry their mediating faith as far as the need exists. Like a pebble breaking the surface of a pond, the healing, mediating arms of one person can reach in circles whose radii span many lengths.

5. Gospel Parallels

Telling

As if they were speaking later to an outside observer, writers of all three versions tell the actions of this pronouncement healing from a distance without any direct quotations.

Setting

Matthew's story summary begins with the action of Jesus' entering Peter's house (Matthew 8:14). Both Mark and Luke give setting to the story that happened after Jesus and the disciples left the synagogue (Mark 1:29 and Luke 4:38).

Disciples And Jesus

For Matthew, Jesus is the focal point. "Jesus" enters the house. "He" sees the mother-in-law. "He" touches her hand. She rises and begins to serve "him" (Matthew 8:14). Of the disciples, Matthew names only Peter. In Luke, Jesus and the disciples interact more than in Mark and Matthew. Luke mentions Simon's name twice. "They" ask him about Simon's mother-in-law. Later, the mother-in-law begins to serve "them." For Mark, the disciples play an important role. Mark names Simon, Andrew, James and John.

Urgency

Prefacing the setting with "as soon as," Mark suggests the importance of going directly to the house. The disciples tell Jesus about the ailing mother-in-law "at once" (Mark 1:30).

In Matthew, Jesus' attention moves directly to the mother-in-law. Jesus immediately surveys the situation and knows what to do. Luke presents a more casual narrative: "After leaving the synagogue" and "Now . . . was suffering from" and "they asked him about her" and "Then" (Luke 4:38-39).

The Healing

Mark and Matthew emphasize the healing touch. In Mark, Jesus comes, takes the woman by the hand, and lifts her up. Then the fever leaves her (Mark 1:31). The healing action includes both taking her by the hand and lifting her up. In Matthew, Jesus touches her hand, the fever leaves her, and then, apparently by her own power, she gets up (Matthew 8:15). See Miracle 7 for a discussion of touch.

Only Luke suggests that Jesus uses words in the healing. He directs his words to the fever. Jesus stands over the woman, he rebukes the fever, the fever leaves her and then she gets up (Luke 4:39). He addresses the fever rather than the woman. He shows power over the fever. He silences the fever. Is the fever the demon whom Jesus does not let speak because the demon knows who Jesus is? Whatever the fever represents, it is an entity separate from the woman. The fever takes the action of leaving the woman.

Mother-in-law

Mark and Matthew describe the woman's trouble as a fever (Mark 1:30 and Matthew 8:14). The physician Luke amplifies this, saying she is "suffering" from a "high" fever (Luke 4:38).

As implied above, according to Matthew and Luke, the woman takes more direct action in her healing by getting up herself when the fever leaves. In all three versions, she wastes no time returning to her work. According to Luke, she rises "immediately" and returns to her task as homemaker and host (Luke 4:39).

Mark 1:31 and Luke 4:39 tell that she begins to serve the disciples as if she were focusing upon her homemaking role. All in one continual sentence, Matthew says Jesus touches her hand, the fever leaves her, she rises and she begins to serve Jesus as if in response to the healing (Matthew 8:15).

---

1. For a fuller discussion, see Brauninger, *Talking With Your Child About Change* (United Church Press, 1994).

Miracle 3

The Leper Healed

Mark 1:40-45 (Matthew 8:1-4; Luke 5:12-16; see Mark 1:35)

---

1. Text

> *A leper came to him begging him, and kneeling he said to him, "If you choose, you can make me clean."*[40] *Moved with pity, Jesus stretched out his hand and touched him, and said to him, "I do choose. Be made clean!"*[41] *Immediately the leprosy left him, and he was made clean.*[42] *After sternly warning him he sent him away at once,*[43] *saying to him, "See that you say nothing to anyone; but go, show yourself to the priest, and offer for your cleansing what Moses commanded, as a testimony to them."*[44] *But he went out and began to proclaim it freely, and to spread the word, so that Jesus could no longer go into a town openly, but stayed out in the country; and people came to him from every quarter.*[45]

2. What's Happening?

First Point Of Action
A leper approaches Jesus and asks Jesus to make him clean.

Second Point Of Action
Jesus heals the man with touch and with words.

Third Point Of Action
The man is cleansed of his leprosy.

Fourth Point Of Action

Jesus warns the man to tell no one about the miracle but to go tell his priest.

Fifth Point Of Action

Instead, the man tells everyone what Jesus did.

Sixth Point Of Action

As a result, Jesus is so deluged by people wanting healing that he no longer stays in town but remains in the country.

3. Connecting Points — Conversations

Interviewing Person Freed Of Leprosy

Asker: Please sit at the table with me awhile. Let us talk about what your healing means. Your body language, that is, your kneeling before Jesus, asked and begged. However, your attitude in approaching Jesus was assertive. You spoke immediately to him. He could heal you, if only he chose, you said. Why did you come to him in this way?

Person Freed Of Leprosy: There was nothing I could do to heal myself. I was little different from a person living with AIDS. Leprosy is the unclean disease of my time. AIDS is the present highest cause of death for Americans aged 25-44 in your time.[1] Some diseases we bring upon ourselves by our own actions. Strangely, they often are the same diseases that come through the innocence of birth or mistakes of transfusion or other medical treatment.

Asker: Do you mean that you carried not only the disease but also the social stigma whether it was your fault or not?

Person Freed Of Leprosy: Yes, the physical effects of leprosy are obvious and ugly. Because the disease is awful, whether leprosy or AIDS, people make victims of those who suffer from it. They make us untouchables. Sufferers become "lepers" rather than "those who have leprosy."

Asker: You have no name in this story.

Person Freed Of Leprosy: How appropriate for me to represent every person with this type of disease. Becoming nameless is also symbolic of the disease. Leprosy eats away at physical identity. Imaginary marques reading "AIDS" replace lifetimes of accomplishments of those outcast people. The sea of persons with AIDS submerges and drowns individual identity.

Asker: You are unlike the leper Naaman. He wanted some dramatics or at least a little fanfare in the healing of his leprosy. You approached Jesus in humility and Jesus healed you immediately. Do you know about Naaman?

Person Freed Of Leprosy: Oh, yes. The great warrior, Naaman, commander of the army of the king of Aram (Syria). He did make quite a fuss. He had leprosy. At the suggestion of the Israelite servant of his wife, Naaman's king had sent him to the king of Israel for healing. He went with horses and chariots, money, many gifts — a superior cleansing offering, I would say. He also carried a letter of introduction telling the king, "You may cure him of his leprosy" (2 Kings 5:6).

Asker: So, like AIDS, leprosy can find its way to almost anyone. What a contrast your story is with that of Naaman. His high profile and his important position did not protect him from leprosy.

Person Freed Of Leprosy: Unfortunately this challenge daunted the king of Israel. He asked who they thought he was, God, or something, to give life or death. Then he recovered enough to think his old enemy was tricking him. (See 2 Kings 5 for the entire story of this Epiphany 6 Old Testament lesson.)

Asker: The king of Israel had no authority. He at least recognized he was powerless to heal Naaman. The prophet Elisha sidestepped the hostility. This mouthpiece for God came to his rescue with a simple cure. I wonder if all that pomp from king to king was telling us that the authority to heal is in a different category than the power to rule a country?

Person Freed Of Leprosy: Could be. Anyway, Naaman sure got angry when Elisha's messenger told him his cure. Washing in the Jordan seven times was too easy and modest for a person of his stature. Besides, were not the waters of his own rivers just as good? Naaman's servants had to talk fast and hard to get him into the River Jordan.

Asker: Yes, and there he went again focusing on artificial, political borders. God's purpose is politically neutral.

Is that not how healing is sometimes? We feel pressed to go to the Mayo Clinic itself — to another place or another authority, when the local general practitioner may be perceptive enough to suggest an effective, unsophisticated remedy. Healing sometimes is simple. Healing sometimes requires doing something basic and doing it for yourself. Jesus did not ask for any payment, that is, sacrificial offering, for healing you.

Person Freed Of Leprosy: Not for himself. God comes as a gift to us. The prophet would not accept payment either. Elisha said he helped Naaman because Elisha served God. Of course, you know what happened to his greedy servant later. Jesus also played by different rules, but he knew the requirements for my society. He sent me to the priest to follow the priest's instructions for a cleansing offering. The priest was the accepted authority on cleansing in my day.

Remember that I had to live away from others. I could not have sat here with you before my cleansing. I could not return home until after the priest gave permission. I needed to go to the priest to fulfill the cleansing and confirm that I was healed. (See Leviticus 13:49 and 14:2-32.)

Asker: Why did you spread the word about your healing after Jesus asked you to be silent?

Person Freed Of Leprosy: Why, you ask? This is why:

> *"O Lord my God, I cried to you for help, and you have*
> *healed me. O Lord, you brought up my soul from Sheol,*
> *restored me to life from among those gone down to the*

Pit. Sing praises to the Lord, O you his faithful ones, and give thanks to his holy name ... To you, O Lord, I cried, and to the Lord I made supplication ... You have turned my mourning into dancing; you have taken off my sackcloth and clothed me with joy" (from Psalm 30, the Psalm for Epiphany 6).

Asker: You were overjoyed at being healed. However, Jesus was stern about your remaining silent. Did you not hear him?

Person Freed Of Leprosy: I got caught up in the moment. This is the surprise, the epiphany of healing. Why do we tell secrets? What compels us to tell something precisely when we are asked not to? I spoke freely to everyone I passed on the way to the priest. I told them all about what happened to me. Is this what those of your time call talk therapy, even if it is to anyone around who will listen? Talking about it helps us to believe reality, even the reality of good news. Perhaps we tell a secret to free ourselves in some way of the burden of holding it in. When should we tell secrets? To spread the good news? Some secrets are too good to keep. As overworked as he was, Jesus knew that.

Interviewing Jesus

Asker: Naaman went away from Elisha's house, saying, "I thought that for me he would surely come out, and stand and call on the name of the Lord his God, and would wave his hand over the spot, and cure the leprosy" (2 Kings 5:11). The man you healed, Jesus, was no commander of a king's army. Your leper was so common he was not even given a name in the story. Neither did you make a big commotion about the situation. You accepted your authority to heal.

Jesus: Unlike the priest, I did not ask first if this person had the means before assigning a certain type of sacrificial offering. Neither a man's name nor a woman's rank should be a factor in healing. God does not play favorites. Unlike those of Naaman's day, I made no grand show of healing. I did not need to shout or carry on in a way that would convince God that God should heal this person. I have the authority to heal.

Asker: You stretched out your hand and touched the man. You met the untouchable. You said a few words. That was it. His healing was simple and immediate.

Jesus: "If you choose, you can make me clean." The gospel writers all quote us exactly. "I do choose. Be made clean!" I did choose. That is all that was necessary for both of us to say.

Asker: The man with leprosy clearly recognized you. He acknowledged your authority. Why is it that often the most simple people see through all the unimportant things? They go right to the core. I talk also with those who are dying. They do not mess around. They get right to the point. That is how your conversation was with the man with leprosy.

Jesus: This fellow came to me by his choice. As far as I know, he had no companion to encourage him. He was a person without a home because of a disease. He was straightforward. He knew what he needed. Without a reservation, he trusted me. I honored him by responding directly to what he said. "If you choose ... I do choose. You can make me clean ... Be made clean."

He approached me with total submission and humility. If I had chosen not to cleanse him, he would have accepted my choice. He received my authority. Simply and without fanfare, this is how our trust in God as parent should be. No extraneous factors need to stand between us.

Asker: I can imagine this person, before coming to you, thinking or talking to himself about how he would approach you. Were his words spontaneous? He was as precise as you. His words must have been the result of much thought. Without doubt, he believed you could cleanse him. You stretched out your hand and touched the man. You used the rituals and the formula, "Be made clean."

Jesus: We have to see the person and the disease. This person was familiar with the formula, the healing rituals of the day. He had been instructed in their importance. He was living in the consequences of their importance. I wonder how many other healers he had approached earlier with these words without response. Perhaps he came only to me because he recognized who I am.

44

Asker: Granted that only one of the three narrators of this healing story said you were moved with pity, Jesus, I wonder about the use of that word this time. Those who related the stories about you generally used the word "compassion," to describe your relationship with the crowds of suffering people. I can recall only three other times that synoptic writers used the word "pity." (See Matthew 18:27, Mark 9:22 and Luke 10:33.) Maybe this is not as important as I am making it. Both words convey that you were moved to help in some way. Pity suggests less empathy and a more distant involvement than compassion. It hints of perfunctory healing.
Jesus: It may have sounded halfhearted to you because I dismissed him immediately. Listen again to the energy present in our brief exchange.

Asker: Turning to your request that the man tell no one about the healing, those who are in the helping or teaching professions empathize with your situation. We give too much. We give ourselves all away. We have nothing left to give. To our horror, we stop caring even though our life, our chosen career, is based on caring relationships.

Today we call this burnout. After a while, we become so protective of what little privacy and energy we have left that we become almost reclusive. How can we honor both responsibilities of sharing the gifts we have in serving others and of taking care of ourselves?
Jesus: Compassion takes its toll on the caregiver. It is tempting to become apathetic when exhausted. You are right. I also am the child of human birth. Everyone was coming to be healed, more than one person could possibly manage. I did not engage the man with leprosy beyond attending to his healing. Those whose services are in great demand wear down in body and spirit. We must pay attention to how we use our energy. More than once I escaped with my disciples for a time of renewal.

Asker: One-on-one relationships require a tremendous outpouring of energy for the professional to remain effective. You were deluged with people wanting to be healed. You could no longer go into town but stayed out in the country. Clergy, schoolteachers, nurses, country doctors — how can we all prevent losing heart?

Jesus: Remember the larger perspective. Remember whose work you are doing and why you are doing it. I continue to do my work because I understand it within the framework of God's work. I know my work will not be finished as long as there are people who suffer. God entrusted to me the power to heal. Remember that I do not try to do it all myself. I, too, delegate. I have given my disciples the power to heal in my name.

No one person is indispensable. We must recognize this as human limitation and not something to feel guilty about. As strange as it may sound, we must learn to forgive ourselves for being human. Then we can accept ourselves as limited and live as fully as possible within those limitations.

4. Words

Leprosy

A familiar disease in Mesopotamia, leprosy is a degenerative skin disease. The skin has areas of white hair and red ulcers. While the Bible avoids calling leprosy a type of sin, ulcerated skin was considered unclean.

Chapters 13 and 14 of Leviticus define the full law from diagnosis by the priest to cleansing and purification rituals. These chapters detail prohibitions: "He shall remain unclean as long as he has the disease; he is unclean. He shall live alone; his dwelling shall be outside the camp" (Leviticus 13:46). Priests also give specific instructions: "The person who has the leprous disease shall wear torn clothes and let the hair of his head be disheveled; and he shall cover his upper lip and cry out, 'Unclean, unclean' " (Leviticus 13:45).

While the disease was associated with uncleanliness, this did not necessarily mean improper hygienic care of the body. Uncleanliness was considered a state of the body and the spirit. According to what a person with leprosy could afford, the priest assigned separate rituals as offerings for cleansing. Below is a sample cleansing offering: "Some of the oil that remains in his hand the priest shall put on the lobe of the right ear of the one to be cleansed, and on the thumb of the right hand, and on the big toe of the right foot, on top of the blood of the guilt offering" (Leviticus 14:17).

Priest

A priest in the New Testament refers to the Jewish priest. The priest was a mediator between the divine and the human. Priests protected the priesthood, sacrifices, and the sacred buildings and vessels from contamination from the unclean. These functions included distinguishing between the holy and the unclean. Priests thought what was unclean was contagious. What was holy essentially was removed from ordinary life and hedged around by the holy.

Priests held authority here. They took seriously the matter of protecting what was holy. The temple of God must not be defiled. Keeping the holy clean and undefiled was a matter of national life and death. The people of Israel must be clean to remain holy. Israel would be doomed to destruction without God's saving presence. Ritual and cleanliness may appear to us to be an obsession by the religious in chapter after chapter of some Old Testament books. Rather, it may have been practical in those days of no refrigeration, and minimal sanitation and disinfectant practices.

Jesus was loyal to the priestly system. He saw both the priesthood and the sacrifices of the temple as within the law. Cleansed persons had to satisfy ceremonial law before returning home. Later, Christianity transferred to Christ himself the role of high priest.

By tradition, priests (plus midwives) were responsible for physical health. The ill saw the physician as one who repairs, who sews together and tends wounds and injuries. The priest-physician was always in demand. Alone in being educated, priests held a position of reverence. The mere presence of a physician offered the hope of relief.

In Egypt, the priesthood contained medical branches. Because people believed illness resulted from evil spirits, magic in religion was important. Use of herbs and the ritualistic repeating of certain words, phrases and sounds of incantations supported the magical dimension of early religion.

In Israel, medical practices marked a significant advance. Early Hebrews threw out magic but kept the herbs as accepted priestly prescriptions. Priest-physicians viewed disease either from a practical standpoint or in terms of the spiritual relationship between the sufferer and God.

By the time of Ecclesiastes, the priest-physician gained prestige as a partner with God. That is, while God is the healer, God has provided medicines to the priest for the cure of sickness. In Jesus' day, priests and prophets closely connected medical functions with religious duties.

Today, while religion and the science of medicine have become distinct fields, hospitals and physicians have recognized the value of hospital chaplaincy as part of the healing team.

Consider, however, the general role of clergy in this decade. Authorities change. Clergy enjoy less prestige partly because of advances in medical science. Clergy no longer carry the weight of being among the few educated persons in society. As authorities have changed, the physical stance of a Roman Catholic priest in the mass reflects a changing role which has also removed clerical distance from worshippers.

Lay people have more access to God. Clergy remove themselves from the clerical pedestal if they have not already fallen off it or been knocked off it in the drive to close the gap between clergy and laity. Ministers are as vulnerable to human frailty as anyone else. In the challenge of the new millennium, ministers also search for authority or reach for new definitions of appropriate, meaningful authority.

Medicine

Does medical science without the art of the spiritual bring healing only of the body and not of the spirit? Is this separation of body and spirit among the causes of spiritual poverty and sickness of the soul? The pendulum's arm swings to New Age music. By floating and disconnecting from the body, listeners engage in an ironic attempt to connect or to reconnect to something nebulous, nameless, and all-encompassing. We separate ourselves from worldly pressures and the world of things. By temporarily moving out into the stars, do we also become lost in them? Can we find in them the awe and completeness of a sense of the whole? Is this need to disconnect visible also in house or condominium cocooning, further evidence of trying to replace one burned-out shell — physical, mental, and spiritual — with the skeletal surroundings of wood or brick? What is medicine for the spirit? When will we enter the age of re-connecting?

Clean, Unclean

The disease of leprosy was connected with the unclean. To be unclean meant to be contaminated by a physical ritual or moral impurity. An impurity might be what is displeasing to the deities or what belongs to the sphere of the demonic. For persons, impurity could come from contact with the discharge of body fluids, as with the oozing wounds of leprosy.

In the Old Testament, holiness and uncleanliness are incompatible. Priests equated cleanliness with holiness. This led to the belief that what was unclean was repulsive to the gods.

Rituals for purification developed. They usually included three stages. First came a waiting period of from one to seven or more days. Second was the use of a cleaning agent such as water or fire. A third requirement was often a sacrifice in the nature of a sin offering. Jesus sent persons healed of leprosy to the priest to make this offering.

A ritual might use water, fire, blood, or a mixture prescribed by the priest as cleansing agents. Water is symbolic of cleansing throughout the Bible. (For more about Jesus and water, see Miracle 2 in the Cycle C volume.) Note the use of water in the healing of Naaman's leprosy. For one-day cleansing, water was the only agent. Blood alone was used to cleanse the altar and holy place. Many sacrifical rituals were sin offerings.

Impurity due to leprosy is a New Testament theme. Within these transitions, the New Testament came to focus almost exclusively on unclean as a moral impurity. The most important of purification rituals related to the day of atonement. Uncleanliness becomes a minor aspect of the doctrine of atonement. Here, to clean means to free from sin and guilt rather than the particulars of ritual uncleanliness. A clean heart is the exclusive work of God. Only God can bring a clean thing out of an unclean. Only Elisha, a representative of God, could heal Naaman.

Note the capacity of Psalm 51 to span the Old and New Testament concepts of clean. See especially "Wash me thoroughly from my iniquity, and cleanse me from my sin" (Psalm 51:2) and "Create in me a clean heart, O God, and put a new and right spirit within me" (Psalm 51:10).

Cleansing was part of the redeeming work of Christ as high priest. Those needing healing were cleansed by his word. Uniquely New Testament and from Jesus was his concern about the inner heart and our inner, moral lives. (See Mark 7:21ff.) He was concerned more about what comes out of us by way of our tongues than what goes in by way of the tongue. In the New Testament, ritual uncleanness gradually gave way to moral laws. Moral law, cleanness from forgiveness, came from outside priestly law.

5. Gospel Parallels

Focus

Luke's version of this healing is refined for storytelling: "Once, when he was in one of the cities, there was a man covered with leprosy" (Luke 5:12). Mark plunges directly into the story. Starting with the leper, Mark tells the story with slightly more emphasis on the leper than on Jesus. Matthew's emphasis falls to the actions of Jesus. Mentioning the "great crowds" that follow Jesus and the "coming down from the mountain" (Matthew 8:1), Matthew puts the story into the perspective of Jesus' ministry. Matthew's focus is on the actions of Jesus.

Man With Leprosy

In Matthew (8:2) and Mark (1:40), the leper approaches Jesus. Luke (5:12) is not as direct, saying that when the man sees Jesus, the man speaks to him. In Matthew and Mark, the man kneels before Jesus. Luke says he "bowed with his face to the ground" (5:12). All three writers assign the same words to the leper; however, in Matthew (8:2) and Luke (5:12) the leper first addresses Jesus as "Lord."

Response Of Jesus

In all three tellings, Jesus stretches out his hand. Matthew is slightly more direct than Mark, who prefaces the action with "Moved with pity" (Mark 1:41), and Luke, who prefaces it with the suggested in-response-to word, "Then" (Luke 5:13). By putting the word formula into the subordinate clause, "saying" (Matthew 8:3), Matthew makes Jesus' action of stretching out his hand and touching the man slightly more important.

The Cleansing

Also in all three tellings, the result is immediate. In Matthew, the passive voice is used (Matthew 8:3), that is, the leprosy is acted upon. It is cleansed. Matthew avoids saying the leprosy leaves the man, as do Mark (1:42) and Luke (5:13). In Mark, the man himself is made clean. Luke omits words about either the leprosy or the man being made clean.

Spreading The Word

Luke reports that Jesus orders the man to tell no one. Luke saves the direct quotation of Jesus' words, the directions to go to the priest and make an offering (Luke 5:14). Matthew is less adamant about telling no one but does include the words in the direct quotation to go to the priest and make an offering (Matthew 8:4).

The Crowds

Luke and Mark report that word is spreading abroad more than ever and crowds gather but Jesus would withdraw to deserted places and pray (Luke 5:15,16). Mark said the healed man freely proclaims the news so Jesus can no longer go into a town openly. People come to him out in the country (Mark 1:45).

---

1. Information from U.S. Agency for International Development as reported in the Lincoln *Journal Star*, August 8, 1995.

51

Miracle 4

Healing The Paralyzed Man

Mark 2:1-12 (Matthew 9:1-8; Luke 5:17-26)

---

1. Text

When he returned to Capernaum after some days, it was reported that he was at home.[1] So many gathered around that there was no longer room for them, not even in front of the door; and he was speaking the word to them.[2] Then some people came, bringing to him a paralyzed man, carried by four of them.[3] And when they could not bring him to Jesus because of the crowd, they removed the roof above him; and after having dug through it, they let down the mat on which the paralytic lay.[4] When Jesus saw their faith, he said to the paralytic, "Son, your sins are forgiven."[5] Now some of the scribes were sitting there, questioning in their hearts,[6] "Why does this fellow speak in this way? It is blasphemy! Who can forgive sins but God alone?"[7] At once Jesus perceived in his spirit that they were discussing these questions among themselves; and he said to them, "Why do you raise such questions in your hearts?[8] Which is easier, to say to the paralytic, 'Your sins are forgiven,' or to say, 'Stand up and take your mat and walk'?[9] But so that you may know that the Son of Man has authority on earth to forgive sins" — he said to the paralytic —[10] "I say to you, stand up, take your mat and go to your home."[11] And he stood up, and immediately took the mat and went out before all of them; so that they were all amazed and glorified God, saying, "We have never seen anything like this!"[12]

2. What's Happening?

First Point Of Action
So many people gather around Jesus when they learn he has returned to Capernaum that there is no room even at the front door for another to enter.

Second Point Of Action
Four people carrying the paralyzed man cannot get into the house. They remove the mat from the roof. The friends dig through the roof, then lower the man down into the house.

Third Point Of Action
Jesus addresses the man, proclaiming that his sins are forgiven.

Fourth Point Of Action
The scribes question Jesus' actions.

Fifth Point Of Action
Jesus speaks to the scribes.

Sixth Point Of Action
Jesus talks to the man again.

Seventh Point Of Action
The man does as Jesus says.

Eighth Point Of Action
The crowd responds and credits God.

3. Connecting Points — Conversations

Interviewing Jesus
Asker: What is this miracle trying to tell us about God?
Jesus: People were waiting for me when I returned home to Capernaum. They were ready and eager to hear the word. This word was different. "I am doing a new thing; now it springs forth"

(Isaiah 43:19) as healing actions in "the wilderness and rivers in the desert" (Isaiah 43:19) where evil likes to roam. You will recognize my authority through the word as I heal by forgiving sin.

I am doing a new thing in a different way. We are moving beyond the priestly game of burnt offerings and other sacrifices. I shall give my life as a final sacrifice. You honor me now by bringing to me your suffering and your sins. "I, I am He who blots out your transgressions for my own sake, and I will not remember your sins" (Isaiah 43:25). (For the entire Cycle B Epiphany 7 reading, see Isaiah 43:18-25.)

Asker: Jesus, I have some confusion about healing and the forgiveness of sin. In the Psalm reading for today, the psalmist connects sin with healing: "The Lord sustains [the poor] on their sickbed; in their illness you heal all their infirmities. As for me, I said, 'O Lord, be gracious to me; heal me, for I have sinned against you' " (Psalm 41:3-4). These verses remind me of your actions in healing the man who was paralyzed. You took action for him when he could not move for himself.

On the one hand, I hear you saying we should not think our illnesses are a punishment from God. When you healed the man with the unclean spirit (Cycle B, Miracle 1), it became clear that while evil exists in this world, God is still superior. I must take responsibility for choosing to follow the positive side rather than succumbing to my dark aspects. In this way, I turn around from thinking I did something wrong to deserve this illness or trouble. God is not using it to punish me. God does not work that way. Instead, I can choose to take responsibility for doing the best I can under the circumstances.

Jesus: I follow you. You must be wondering how the concept of sin fits into this.

Asker: Exactly. It still sounds as if the trouble somehow were my fault.

Jesus: As you will see in other healing miracles, there are different causes for illness. Look, for example, at the person with the withered hand (Cycle B, Miracle 5) and the person with the hearing/

55

speaking impairment (Cycle B, Miracle 8). Some problems are purely organic; others are psychogenic in origin.

When suffering people come to me, I pay attention to the whole person. Sometimes the condition of the soul presents a block to healing. Other paralysis is clearly physical in origin, as with severing of a spinal nerve. By the way, I consider the work being done now in your country to be just as much a miracle as my healing work.

Asker: Are you referring to the research in making a bridge at the genetic, DNA level of life between the severed pieces of a spinal chord?

Jesus: Yes, I believe God is still creating, as the spirit is present in the creative human mind. God is still involved in progress. Now, back to our conversation.

When the four men lowered the paralyzed man through the ceiling of the house, I saw that he needed forgiveness. The alienation he endured, that is, the break in his relationship with God had to be healed before the paralysis of his body would release him.

Asker: You responded to the faith of the four men who brought him to you, but you addressed him directly.

Jesus: These four men gave the greatest acknowledgment of my authority as a healer and offerer of forgiveness that one could give. Acting on their faith that I could help, they brought me a suffering friend. They showed the strength of their faith by risking the ridicule or scorn of others to dig a hole in the roof of another person's house. In your day, not many would do this for fear of instant litigation.

Asker: You called the suffering man "son." Is that because he was younger than you? Were you acknowledging that all are children of God and that you spoke in the name of God?

Jesus: I called him a son as I called the woman with the bleeding malady a daughter. (See Cycle B, Miracle 7.) I did this with the hope of communicating that they were already reconnected. As soon as I spoke to the man, God brought him back into relationship through forgiveness. This is also why I called myself the Son of Man. I am a bridge between God and humanity. I, too, am a child of God.

When we fall out of relationship with God, we feel so far away that our prayers seem to wander lost in some canyon as a distant whisper. Yet, it is we who are distant, not God. God stands waiting all along for us to approach. God is accessible. When we bring our suffering and our alienation that need forgiveness, God stands ready to receive and forgive. To call sufferers sons or daughters reminds them of the union we share with our Holy Parent.

Asker: Only later, after you responded to the questioning of the scribes, did you tell the paralyzed man to pick up his mat and go home. When you did so, your words to him, "I say to you," carried a silent "but" before them.

Jesus: An indirect purpose of this healing shows the scribes and all other witnesses that Jesus, the Son of Man, has the authority to forgive sins. The "but" indicates a change of the old rules that stood in the way of the law of love. Do you hear the subtle play on words with the double meaning of paralysis? With the paralysis of relationships, we become unable to say the words we need to say and to do those things we need to do.

I am doing a new thing by challenging the rules that interfere and by offering alternate ways out of paralysis of this nature. You and I will speak of this again when we visit about the healing of the man with the withered hand. (See Cycle B, Miracle 5.) We must constantly remind each other of each person's value.

Interviewing The Paralyzed Man

Asker: You never said a word in this miracle. You stood up, immediately picked up your mat, and walked out before everyone.

Paralyzed Man: I did not approach Jesus with words. Silence was part of my paralysis. My friends recognized this. They realized they had to act for me. Not only did I need their help with mobility, I also needed to receive their neighborliness. They showed their ability to love a neighbor as themselves.

57

Asker: Will you tell me what it was like to be paralyzed?

Paralyzed Man: You were telling me yesterday about a woman you knew who had a frozen arthritic shoulder. Pain, not ice, froze her shoulder just as the pain of my soul froze me. You said the living tissue in her shoulder grew together like strips of Velcro. The tissue had to be pulled apart before she could move it again. Her physical therapy amounted to thawing the paralysis with the deep heat of moist, hot packs and the penetrating vibrations, what did you call them?

Asker: Ultrasound. It promotes movement and healing at the cellular level. Even as my friend's healing process began, her exercise and rehabilitation required the help of another person. She still could take no action herself. She said she would will her shoulder to move. It was as immobile as concrete.

Paralyzed Man: I also was a passive receiver of help. As the physical therapist manipulated your friend's shoulder, the woman slowly became able herself to move through a range of motion exercises. I was able to get up and walk home.

Asker: I wonder what state of alienation or sin froze you into physical and emotional inaction? What thawed your paralysis? Was it a kind word, a feeling of being understood?

Paralyzed Man: It was feeling that I was forgiven deep in the cellular level of my soul. Jesus understood completely. It was okay. It was the persistence of four friends in taking action when I could not move myself.

Asker: Jesus told you to get up and go to your home. Is that why you said nothing but headed, singlemindedly, out the door?

Paralyzed Man: Jesus freed me. What better gratitude could I show but to exercise my freedom to move? I returned to living my life.

Interviewing One Of The Four Who Carried The Paralyzed Man

Asker: You went to a great deal of trouble for your paralyzed friend. You must have cared about him. You were not to be deterred. Why did you not just wait to bring him to Jesus until another time when the crowds around Jesus were smaller?

Carrier: There was no time for waiting. Jesus was there. We could not miss him.

Asker: Did you ask permission to dig through the hard-packed clay into the roof of the house? What does this say about trespassing or breaking a law for the sake of a healing?

Carrier: We did trespass in our enthusiasm and urgency. Surely, we would repair the hole later. This was not necessarily the home of a stranger. What is more important, the possible healing of a suffering person or a repairable hole in a roof?

Asker: Then this is a lesson in friendship and the importance of one human being. It is also a matter of Jesus showing his authority to the scribes by bridging God and humanity with the healing of forgiveness.

Carrier: They are all tied together. It is a lesson in faith as well as friendship. We who carried our friend to Jesus had a clear faith in Jesus as a healer.

Interviewing A Scribe

Asker: You were not actually talking aloud, but Jesus could easily guess what the questioning was in your hearts.

Scribe: Jesus understands our purpose. The most important phrase in our questioning is that it is in our hearts. It is not just head talk. Our concern for preserving the law is real. Always, we think first of the laws. It is our life and our purpose as scribes to protect the law.

Asker: I read the psalmist's words for today and think of your response to Jesus: "My enemies wonder in malice when I will die, and my name perish. And when they come to see me, they utter empty words, while their hearts gather mischief; when they go out, they tell it abroad. All who hate me whisper together about me; they imagine the worst for me." (See Psalm 41:5-7 from Cycle B, Epiphany 7.)

Scribe: When the man stood up and went out before us, we were amazed. We did glorify God.

59

Asker: Nevertheless, in your hearts you continue to gather mischief.
Scribe: We continue to gather mischief.

4. Words

House

In Palestine, the earliest known houses were the mud houses of Jericho. Most houses were in cities, towns, or villages. The house was mainly a shelter from the dangers of night and from foul weather. Their thick walls also offered comfort. During the time of Israel and Judah, houses were smaller with thinner walls and were generally not as well built.

Houses were rectangular and most likely faced a street. They adjoined other houses. A house may have been part of the city wall with a window opening to the outside. The door was wood with one horizontal beam and two uprights. Of the three rooms, families used one for domestic animals, another for sleeping quarters, and a central room for cooking and heating. Smoke went out through the open, latticed window.

The ceiling was made of wooden beams plastered over with clay. Steps would lead to a guest room in the roof. The surface of the clay roof regularly needed rolling and renewing. When the carriers of the paralyzed man dug an entry through the roof and ceiling, they caused an inconvenience. However, they did not ruin the house. Still, their act was dramatic.

Son Of Man

"Son of Man" is a term for a human being. We are all children of man and woman. Son of Man was also a title for Jesus. "Son of" reveals a connection or affinity with someone. The title is always found in words attributed to Jesus himself. It draws one toward Jesus with a sense of kinship with ordinary humanity.

Matthew uses the phrase in 27 verses. Mark uses it thirteen times. Luke attributes the term to Jesus 25 times. The uppercase Son suggests the title means more than human. The Son of Man is also the Son of God. Might the uppercase Son emphasize the special relationship Jesus had with God? Expanding this further, we are all Children of God because of the special relationship we share with God and God holds with us through Jesus.

Writers of *The Interpreter's Dictionary Of The Bible, Volume 4,*[1] suggest that since the Gospel called Mark holds particular importance, students might pay close attention to Mark's highly developed concept of the Son of Man. First, it is Jesus' designation for himself. Second, the term contains predictions of the passion. That is, Jesus is a person who must suffer, know rejection, die and rise again.

Since Son of Man was Semitic, the term would be familiar to those who followed Jesus. Some historians suppose that Jesus may have left it to his hearers to puzzle out the meaning of this phrase. Others suggest the later church inserted the term. Given his humble nature, Jesus may not have used it to describe himself.

In the nine miracles of Cycle C, Jesus twice refers to himself as the Son of Man. In the present miracle, writers assign the term to Jesus. This reveals Jesus' authority on earth to forgive sins. In the opening of the fifth miracle of Cycle B, the man with the withered hand, Jesus also addresses the issue of his authority. Responding to scribes challenging him for plucking grain on the sabbath, Jesus says that "the Son of Man is lord even of the sabbath" (Mark 2:28).

Demon

In biblical days, demon was the term given to the cause of whatever bad happened to a person's body or mind. A demon is an evil being, the devil, an inferior divinity. It is a persistently tormenting person, force, or passion. Torment suggests great physical pain or mental anguish. The devil, a subordinate evil spirit, is the major spirit of evil and is the foe of God.

In order to define and understand fully, a concept, students look at its antithesis. By looking at the opposite of God, does one give the devil, if not an identity, at least a presence that competes with God? We might throw out the idea of devil as anthropomorphism, that is, evil in the shape of a human. However, evil still exists as a force opposing good.

61

Do devil worship and satanic cults today symbolize supreme rebellion? Beyond fascination with the macabre, practicers of devil worship delve into the mystery of the dark side. Some individuals are drawn to what they fear. Devil worship also assumes less obvious forms. Some people seem to thrive on chaos. Chaos stimulates them. When things settle down, they are not happy until they have stirred up chaos again.

If a demon is a symbol of chaos, where is the chaos and disorder in our lives? Who and what are our specific demons? What are the struggles with the baffling, negative factors affecting our lives? What are the clear, understandable negative forces? What issues do you fight against that continually reappear in your community, work, or life?

Does a demon gain its power because we cannot touch, see, or hear it? Are how we allow evil to influence our attitudes and the way we behave the greater harms? What does forgiveness do to evil or to our capacity to coexist with the negative forces around and within us?

Consider that demons, objects of pagan worship, were said to inhabit waste places and ruins. Jesus went to the wastelands and into human deserts where people were isolated and left vulnerable to demonic influence. When the devil tempted Jesus in the wilderness, Jesus met evil head on. He stood up to it. From the beginning, evil forces "knew" with whom they were dealing.

We have the present challenge of identifying and entering the erratic wastelands where our people are vulnerable. Among them are the stairways of trashy apartments hiding in small towns. Transient kids wander lost in new schools. Middle-aged parents lose their souls to a commuting race with only a radio talk show for community.

Now, as then, we can expel negative spirits by meeting them with the stronger force of God. People in pagan times wore amulets and charms to ward off evil spirits. Good luck charms or painting the door blue to send demons away is a carryover from earlier times. More than announcing we are Christian, does the wearing of a cross necklace offer a similar, positive symbol? Where is the line between superstition and faith? Is the basis of superstition negative and the formation of faith positive?

Demonism

Demonism externalizes human experience by projecting it. Persons with a troubled spirit sometimes assign their troubles to spirits outside themselves. Persons see disease as the result of an external, demonic hand rather than an organic disorder.

If we curse the devil when something bad happens and thank God when something good happens, are both projections? This is a puzzle. It is also a choice. Giving God priority, Christians choose hope even in the midst of despair. We do not give equal rank to two gods, a good god and a bad god. Sickness or trouble just happens. Some trouble we can prevent, some we cannot. No matter what the terminology, Jesus comes with the message that the light wins out over the darkness. God is a God of love and compassion.

Spirit

In the early mind, demons and spirit existed side by side. People believed Yahweh sent an evil spirit of the demon to produce sickness. In pagan times, no clear distinction existed between the demonic and the disease. They saw noxious, unclean spirits as spirits of delirium and melancholy producing physical or psychic disorders. They saw Jesus as a gifted person. He proved himself more powerful than the unholy spirits that people believed poisoned their lives. Establishing his authority as a bringer of healing and of the good spirit was important to his ministry.

"Spirit" carries two meanings. It is an impersonal influence, as intangible as breath or the blowing wind. Yet, like the wind, we see its effects. Some winds bring good, some carry harm. We wonder which is by whim and which by design. Wind bears the germs of some diseases. It also brings nourishing seasonal rains.

The second meaning sees spirit as a physical manifestation of unembodied personalities taking up temporary lodging in a person. Perhaps negative spirits only take up temporary lodging. As part of God's caring design at creation, God's spirit is permanently within each of us and goes with us as Emmanuel (Matthew 1:23).

Each time worshippers sing "The Doxology," we hear the invitation to ponder the meaning of Holy Spirit. In recent years, some worship traditions have emphasized God's triune nature as

Creator, Redeemer, and Sanctifier. This further unveils the meaning of Holy Spirit.

To sanctify is to set apart for holy use, to make holy, and to purify. A sanctuary is a holy, sacred place. We respect the human body as a sanctuary for our soul. God is the Spirit more powerful than the unholy demons. As Sanctifier, Jesus carries and leaves with us the Spirit that makes things holy. When Jesus dies, God does not desert us but provides a sustaining presence.

Forgiveness

Jesus deliberately forgave sins. He taught that obedience to God must always take precedence over mere political expedience. He claimed that all authority was his and gave his followers the right to become children of God.

Forgiveness is an act of God by which God graciously takes away the obstacles that separate us. Complete forgiveness grants pardon without harboring resentment. It opens the way for the free "try again" of grace. It makes way for fellowship and neighborliness because it focuses on hope and on the possibilities we carry as human beings.

Sin destroys relationships of community with God and humankind. This all broadens the meaning of repentance for sin. When we feel forgiven, we are able to forgive others. Blocked relationships reopen. Wholeness becomes the healing of the soul and the consequent recovery of power in life.

Healing frees us from whatever catches us in the paralysis of inaction. Forgiveness restores our strength because once-paralyzed energy is available again for productive use. Healing frees us for living.

A symbol of this freedom is the implicit message, "You are free to go now and be about living." This message is a common form of forgiveness in the New Testament. In the present miracle, Jesus tells the man to head for home. When he healed Simon Peter's mother-in-law, he took her hand, lifting her up off the bed so she could continue her work. (See Cycle B, Miracle 2.)

In the third miracle of this cycle, Jesus sent the healed leper on to the priest to take the next step. He stilled the storm so they could continue their journey across the lake (Cycle B, Miracle 6). He told the woman with the bleeding disorder to go in peace. He told Jairus' daughter to get up so she could walk around. Then he reminded her parents to get on with caring for her by getting her something to eat (Cycle B, Miracle 7). Jesus told Bartimaeus, "Go" (Cycle B, Miracle 9).

5. Gospel Parallels

Setting The Stage

The Gospel called Matthew mentions only that some people were carrying the man on a bed (Matthew 9:2). Mark and Luke go into great detail setting the stage for the healing. Both emphasize the crowd that prevented entry through the door, the alternate route through the roof, and letting down the mat (Mark 2:4) or the bed (Luke 5:19).

Mark draws attention to the crowd first, suggesting Jesus' popularity. Then Mark, the most specific writer, refers to four of the men who carry the paralyzed man. Mark suggests the effort necessary to "remove the roof" and "having dug through it." Luke refers to the men coming with the paralyzed man and only mentions the crowd in passing (Luke 5:19). Luke suggests slightly less expenditure of effort in saying that they go up on the roof and let him down "through the tiles." Luke (5:19) says they let down his bed "into the middle of the crowd in front of Jesus" — no back-in-a-corner for these people but right where Jesus could not miss the man.

Role Of Faith

In all three versions, Jesus responds to "their" faith (Mark 2:5, Matthew 9:2 and Luke 5:20), that is, the faith of the people who bring the man to him. Perhaps "their" faith includes the paralytic. It was he whom Jesus addresses. In Mark and Luke, Jesus calls the man "son." In Luke, he addresses him as "friend." In all three versions, he says the man's sins are forgiven. Mark prefaces the words with these: "Take heart." Luke adds "you" to the words.

Response Of Scribes (And Pharisees)

In none of the versions do the scribes refer to Jesus by name. Mark says "this fellow" (Mark 2:6). Matthew says "this man" (Matthew 9:3). Luke, placing an even greater emotional distance, reports a common response by both "the scribes and the Pharisees." Luke says, "Who is this who …?" (Luke 5:21).

Matthew briefly summarizes the scribes' response (Matthew 9:3). Again, speaking from greater distance, Luke says the scribes and the Pharisees "began to question" (Luke 5:21). Mark pays more attention to the seriousness of the questioning. They question not as mental sport but "in their hearts" (Mark 2:6-7).

All three writers refer to blasphemy; however, Matthew 9:3 and Mark 2:7 declare the healing as blasphemy. Luke, less emphatic on blasphemy, focuses on the "who" (Luke 5:21). Mark 2:7 and Luke 5:21 add "Who can forgive sins but God alone?" These words add another aspect, connecting the man's paralysis with sin.

Jesus' Response To The Scribes And Pharisees

Mark details taking note of the scribes first in verse 6 and again in verse 8. First, Mark comments that they were questioning "in their hearts" (Mark 2:7). After they asked their questions, Jesus "at once . . . perceived in his spirit that they were discussing these questions among themselves" (Mark 2:8). In Luke, Jesus again "perceived their questionings" (Luke 5:22), and in Matthew, he perceived "their thoughts" (Matthew 9:4).

Jesus addresses the scribes directly. In Mark, he asks, "Why do you raise such questions in your hearts?" (Mark 2:8). In Matthew, he asks, "Why do you think evil in your hearts?" (Matthew 9:4) In Luke, he asks, "Why do you raise such questions in your hearts?" (Luke 5:22)

The next lines are similar in all three Gospels. Jesus asks them further, "Which is easier, to say to the paralytic, 'Your sins are forgiven,' or to say, 'Stand up and take your mat and walk'? But so that you may know that the Son of Man has authority on earth to forgive sins…" (Mark 2:9,10) Matthew's and Luke's words are the same except they omit Mark's "to the paralytic" and "take your mat and."

Jesus' Next Words To The Paralyzed Man

Mark relates: " — he said to the paralytic — 'I say to you, stand up, take your mat and go to your home' " (Mark 2:10,11). Matthew says, "he *then* said" and instead of "mat" he says, "bed" (Matthew 9:6). Luke says, " — he said to the one who was paralyzed" (Luke 5:24).

Response Of The Healed Man

In all three narratives, the man stands up. In Mark and Luke, he stands up immediately. (See Mark 2:12 and Luke 5:25.) Matthew condenses the action, saying simply that he went to his home. Mark says he "took the mat and went out before all of them "(Mark 2:12). Luke gives the greatest detail: "Immediately he stood up before them, took what he had been lying on, and went to his home, glorifying God" (Luke 5:25).

Response Of The Crowd

In Mark, the crowd is "amazed and glorified God" (Mark 2:12). Luke says, "Amazement seized all of them, and they glorified God and were filled with awe" (Luke 5:26).

Matthew does not quote the crowd but directly connects the response of the crowd with the issue of authority: "When the crowds saw it, they were filled with awe, and they glorified God, who had given such authority to human beings" (Matthew 9:8).

Mark and Luke quote the crowd: "'We have never seen anything like this" (Mark 2:12) and "We have seen strange things today" (Luke 5:26).

---

1. See George A. Buttrick, Ed., *The Interpreter's Dictionary Of The Bible,* Volume 4 (Nashville: Abingdon Press, 1962).

Miracle 5

The Withered Hand

Mark 2:23—3:6 (Matthew 12:9-14; Luke 6:6-11)

---

1. Text

One sabbath [Jesus] was going through the grain-fields; and as they made their way his disciples began to pluck heads of grain.[23] The Pharisees said to him, "Look, why are they doing what is not lawful on the sabbath?"[24] And he said to them, "Have you never read what David did when he and his companions were hungry and in need of food?[25] He entered the house of God, when Abiathar was high priest, and ate the bread of the Presence, which it is not lawful for any but the priests to eat, and he gave some to his companions."[26] Then he said to them, "The sabbath was made for humankind, and not humankind for the sabbath;[27] so the Son of Man is lord even of the sabbath."[28]

Again he entered the synagogue, and a man was there who had a withered hand.[3:1] They watched him to see whether he would cure him on the sabbath, so that they might accuse him.[2] And he said to the man who had the withered hand, "Come forward."[3] Then he said to them, "Is it lawful to do good or to do harm on the sabbath, to save life or to kill?" But they were silent.[4] He looked around at them with anger; he was grieved at their hardness of heart and said to the man, "Stretch out your hand." He stretched it out, and his hand was restored.[5] The Pharisees went out and immediately conspired with the Herodians against him, how to destroy him.[6]

69

2. What's Happening?

The Gospel called Mark portrays Jesus as a man of action. If God is to be with us, Emmanuel, then God is a God of action. Jesus had the capacity to use the moment to teach through his actions. We meet him in the middle of doing his work. This healing story also follows the form of a pronouncement story. Jesus confronts a charge or a controversial situation. The plot builds to a climax in which Jesus speaks an authoritative pronouncement. Sympathetic with similar issues that the early church faced, the story suggests that Jesus, also, does not deserve the treatment he receives.

First Point Of Action
Jesus enters the grainfield so his disciples can obtain food. He feeds them because they are hungry. The Pharisees question Jesus about working on the sabbath. Jesus answers the Pharisees with a story from their common scripture. Jesus gives a new, double pronouncement teaching.

Second Point Of Action
Jesus enters the synagogue. So they might accuse Jesus, the Pharisees watch him to see if he will attempt to cure on the sabbath. Jesus addresses the man with the withered hand. He helps the man because the man is hurting. Aware that the Pharisees are observing him, Jesus speaks another pronouncement as a question. The Pharisees are silent. Also silent, Jesus responds with emotion to their attitude.

Third Point Of Action
Jesus commands the man with the withered hand to stretch out his hand. The man does as Jesus directs. God acts, restoring the man's hand.

Fourth Point Of Action
The Pharisees respond by leaving and conspiring with the Herodians about how to destroy Jesus.

3. Connecting Points — Conversations

Interviewing The Person With The Withered Hand

In some healing miracles, the suffering person speaks. The man with the withered hand does not speak. We never know whether the silence means a total lack of faith, trust, or some de-gree of faith. Yet the man has voice in his presence. He speaks by his being where he will meet Jesus. He is at the synagogue.

Asker: Who are you, man with the withered hand?

Person: Though neither the editor Mark nor Jesus calls me by name, I have a name. I am a person, not only an example of Jesus making a point.

Asker: What do you mean?

Person: You might also be a Pharisee looking for wrongdoing on the sabbath. For Jesus, even with my withered hand I do count for more than obedience to the Law, including that of doing no work on the sabbath.

Asker: How do we know this?

Person: You cannot know from a distance, but I can tell you this. Whether you stood waiting and expecting or huddled in a corner of despair, if Jesus singled you out, if Jesus looked you in the eye and you looked into his eyes, if Jesus commanded you, however quietly, "Come forward," and then, as you stood before him, he said to you, "Stretch out your hand," you would know which Jesus believed to be the higher law, showing compassion and mercy to one of God's creation or not working on the sabbath. Jesus puts the person first.

Asker: Healers were a denarius a dozen in your day. Why was this man Jesus so different?

Person: Would ordinary healers jeopardize themselves by blatantly breaking the Law? Jesus did call himself the Son of Man. He was more than the ordinary healer.

Asker: Why does your withered hand make you special?

Person: In this age, I am useless, vulnerable and dependent. With

71

only one good hand, I could not be a mason, a fisher, or a carpenter, or engage in any other trade. I cannot make a living. I cannot take care of a family. It is I who must be taken care of.

Asker: So why do you come to the synagogue? Those who beg stand outside the city gate.
Person: From your perspective, it is unclear if I come reluctantly or faithfully or if today is my first trip to the synagogue. There is nothing wrong with my feet. I can walk. On the other hand, to bring myself here, I might have needed some persuasion. I might have lost heart through these years of constant struggle.

You may also ask if the Pharisees planted me in the synagogue. Am I here because I, or they, knew Jesus was coming?

Asker: Is it a case of being in the right place at the right time?
Person: My only real action in the synagogue is making myself available. All any of us can do is to be available to receive the gift of healing. Healing is always a surprise, always a gift. We can neither command nor wishfully think healing to come. When healing does happen, we simply must stretch out our hand to receive it. I speak by extending my hand. I am a recipient of healing.

Person: Now, let me ask you, who are you as you look at me? Do you see a beggar who has given up or a person who is ready to be made whole? Do you see one who, for you, has become dehumanized and worthless because of a withered hand? Do you see someone waiting to get on with life? What do you see in this impairment I carry? For you, do I still count as a human being?

Person: You live in a different time. You have surgeries that can correct some hand abnormalities. You have prostheses. You have job opportunities that can minimize the need for hand labor.

What is the withering of your own hand? What does it mean for you in your day? In what way has your hand become shriveled or lost its energy, its power? That is, what about your incapacity to be mentally, physically, or emotionally productive? What is the ongoing or chronic nature of a symbolic withered hand in your life? Do you want to change it enough that you would stretch it out and offer, that is, allow God to transform it? It would change your entire life. Would that be too scary? Would you prefer to carry the impediments of a withered hand?

When we are hurting, why do we go to the synagogue or church? Is our going passive or active? Is it more than from devotional habit? What is the parishioner looking for, needing, hungering for? What comfort or challenge can we as preachers offer? When is the challenge a comfort? When does the comfort become a challenge?

How do we bring ourselves into the presence of what can help us? When we bring ourselves to God, is the coming in spite of ourselves and our sense of defeat? Are we responding to the hope of God beyond ourselves?

Interviewing A Pharisee
The Pharisees reflect the Jewish preoccupation with the Law.
Asker: When is it okay to break the Law?
Pharisee: You ask that without comprehending that the letter of the Law is just about all we have left of our religion. Political tension is tight. Everything is falling apart. Foreign practices have invaded our people with all sorts of corruption.

It is never okay to break the Law. The Law is more than just a set of regulations. It is a way of life; it binds us together wherever we are. We go wrong in not obeying God's commandments.

Asker: Why do you hound Jesus?
Pharisee: We are just doing what we think is right, following the precise meaning of the Law, following the law of our religion. From our perspective, it is Jesus who is out of line. We have a duty to keep an eye on him at all times.

Asker: Why do you follow Jesus into the synagogue?
Pharisee: The synagogue is the gathering point of Jewish life and thought. It is our coming together as Jewish people, our identity — national and religious. How dare Jesus break the sabbath with his healing, especially in the synagogue?

73

Now, we do make exceptions. If the man with the withered hand were in immediate danger of his life, the rules allow for healing. In this person's circumstances, waiting one more day would not have threatened his life.

Asker: Do you not think Jesus knew that? Healing the man quietly on another day would not have made his point that there is a new law, a new way of doing things.

I hear your silence. How else do you speak? Where is your voice?

Pharisee: We speak with the words of a question. We ask Jesus directly in the wheat field why the disciples are doing what is unlawful on the sabbath.

Asker: How else does your silence speak?

Pharisee: Silence can be a powerful threat. We observe Jesus. We want to make him uneasy. We watch him in the synagogue to see whether he will cure the man with the withered hand on the sabbath. We gather evidence so we might accuse Jesus.

Asker: You are so intent on the Law that you miss the whole point that God loves each person. Jesus even draws on the sagas of your religion, the story of David entering the temple because his men were hungry and eating the priest's food. There is much evidence to support such compassion.

Pharisee: We speak with the silence of satisfaction. We have the evidence to nail Jesus. As his superiors, we do not need to respond to Jesus or answer to him. His actions condemn him.

Asker: Are you silent because Jesus truly disturbs you by his uncanny ability to ask the key questions though he knows they will get him into trouble? The issue is not your threatening him. This Jewish brother challenges your entire view of your relationship with God. You were silent when he said to you, "Is it lawful to do good or to do harm on the sabbath, to save life or to kill?" Now you are silent in response to my question. I wonder what answer you will give in your heart.

74

Asker: Finally, you speak by your actions. After the miracle, you simply leave, walk out.

Pharisee: We are building our case. We have our evidence. More words are unnecessary.

Asker: As present-day preachers and church members, when are you a Pharisee? How do you talk with Jesus? When are you closed-minded? How do you show your unwillingness to grow? When is it easier to focus on nitpicking than to face change?

Interviewing Jesus

Jesus has the capacity to use the moment to do his teaching. This encourages the preacher's awareness of the everyday. We also can use available moments of learning and teaching.

Asker: The man with the withered hand has a chronic condition and may have become comfortable as a victim. Why do you single him out for healing?

Jesus: This is even more reason for choosing him. Consider the silence of acceptance, adjustment, or coming to terms with a chronic condition. Do not confuse this with inconvenience or the apparent absence of suffering. They are only necessary ways of putting up with what is broken to carry on with life.

Have you ever felt so strongly someone's presence, someone's wordlessly calling to you from the heart, that you turned to address that person? In a room filled with people, have you ever observed someone who appeared vulnerable? Have you then approached that person with the intent of drawing out or somehow assisting her or him? Did you see the sufferer's surprise?

People who suffer do not have to wave both arms in the air to get my attention. That is the last thing someone who lives with a seemingly unchangeable condition would do. Strangers see only the problem rather than recognizing a person's full identity.

It is better that the man suffering from a withered hand does not seek me out. I am not called to respond first to his asking. I can make the point directly about the purpose of sabbath. My action toward this person becomes entirely my looking out for him, my initiative.

God is present. Our Sustainer walks with us through suffering. While we turn to God, God also comes to us when God sees our need.

Asker: When you stand as intermediary in the healing rebirth of the man with the withered hand, you speak directly with an authoritative voice. You say, "Come forward" and "Stretch out your hand." Why are you so brief?
Jesus: I speak simply. A command is clear and direct. I see and acknowledge the suffering and need not waste time interrogating the sufferer. Why prolong suffering? Why use the whole sabbath when the work of sabbath healing may require only minutes?

Asker: Why do you heal him on the sabbath?
Jesus: It appears that to hold up his healing one more day will make no critical difference to his longstanding condition. An outsider cannot fully know the circumstances. Why would God want anyone to suffer another minute for any reason if God could alleviate that suffering? God wishes well for us.

Asker: Regarding the juxtaposition of these stories, the sabbath question and healing this man on the sabbath, why focus on the sabbath?
Jesus: Everything related to the sabbath has become, "Do not do this" and "Do not do that." The sabbath is a special day, a holy day, and a life-giving day. God created and gave light to the world on the first day of creation's week.

Is there anything more life-giving than healing or enabling one of God's human creatures to function as wholly as possible? The smile of God's heart broadens when one child is healed or brought to more fullness of living on sabbath day.

Asker: What do you tell us about who God is in this miracle?
Jesus: If God is to be with us, Emmanuel, then God is a God of action. God puts people first. God is in charge. God has a clear record of bringing order to chaos. God stays present with us in the middle of the chaos — global, disease, personal, relational. God also is present in the solutions.

76

However, just as I weep when my friend dies, so do I weep with you for having unexpected limits put on you beyond the usual limits of a human being — particularly when they are not fixable. Therefore, when God can make a difference, God does not wait for Monday when healing can happen Sunday.

Asker: You do not ignore the Pharisees. You address them directly.
Jesus: My purpose is not to hide but to illumine. I do not intend to close off from life but to open for life.

Asker: You address the Pharisees directly, making two pronouncements. What do you mean by "The sabbath was made for humankind, and not humankind for the sabbath"? Your words are a direct contradiction to the Law.
Jesus: I wonder what is necessary for men and women to grasp how deeply God loves them, how intimately God knows us and stands with us in all things. How ironic it is that current tradition allows us to save an animal, essentially for economic reasons, on the sabbath. Yet by condemning a human being to death for breaking some sabbath laws, we place people in a position inferior to animals.

Asker: Why do you add, "So the Son of Man is lord even of the sabbath"?
Jesus: Maybe I did not add it. What I do know is that I speak and act with an inner authority. Quietly and sometimes noisily, someone has to get things straightened out here. I believe God sent me to do the job. It is God who is in charge.

Asker: When the Pharisees challenge your leading your disciples into the wheat field, why do you tell them the story of David?
Jesus: I am a descendant of the house of David. I, too, am a Jew. David was looking out for his hungry companions. His story offers a precedent.

Our Creator takes care of creation. I take care of the disciples. First comes human need, then adherence to the Law. There are exceptions to the Law that transcend it. I challenge the Pharisees to rethink the place they give to rigid regulations. They have lost sight of the relationship between God and humanity.

Asker: Your second pronouncement comes as a question: "Is it lawful to do good or to do harm on the sabbath, to save life or to kill?" Why did you state it as a question?

Jesus: A question invites exchange. This question focuses on the basic issue of sabbath. We change and grow only as we ourselves address issues.

Asker: Is that why the response of the Pharisees is silence, because the sandal fits?

Jesus: Silence also speaks. The question sets them to thinking.

Asker: Your silence also speaks. When they do not answer, Mark reports that you are both angry and saddened.

Jesus: These are emotions of a human being, a son of man. I, too, become frustrated. I, too, wonder at the impossibility of my task as God's messenger. My task is to show by my actions what God is like and how we reflect God by our actions and our relationships with each other.

Asker: Jesus, what about all the others who are not singled out for healing?

Jesus: Those who are not obviously healed should not feel God is abandoning them. Healing comes in all forms, as inner whispers of encouragement and a sensing of God's sustaining presence in suffering and in restoration and rehabilitation. God comes as an idea for finding another way of accomplishing a task when an obstacle hinders our doing it.

Even when we give up on ourselves, God does not give up on us. When God created the world, God did not say, "I'm all done now. That's forever." God remains active in our lives.

4. Words

Abiathar

The name Abiathar, meaning "the father (God) gives abundantly," has interesting connotations for this story because one of Jesus' emphases is that of a giving God. However, biblical scholars think some genealogical references were based on a mistake about which priest was the son of whom, Abiathar or Ahimelech. Also associated with the Old Testament pericope is the suggestion that Abiathar was the last of the family of the priest Eli, who trained Samuel. For more information, refer to these names in *The Interpreter's Dictionary*.

The assigned epistle in which Paul speaks of treasures in clay vessels brings a third connection with the story. David asks and receives holy bread for his men from his high priest (1 Samuel 21). David says not only priests but "the vessels of the young men are holy" (verse 5). Perhaps all people, though made of breakable clay, are valuable vessels and vehicles for expressing God and receiving healing from God.

Suppose that, as a growing boy, Jesus read the story about Samuel's call (1 Samuel 3:1-10) and reread it at the time he performed miracles. Jesus could have wondered about and pondered the same questions Samuel must have considered, that is, who was calling to him and what God was asking him. Anyone who observed Jesus at work also could have asked these questions. Could these be our questions today: Who calls me? How do I know if this call is legitimate? Would I respond as affirmatively and wholeheartedly to the call were I to learn that it is not someone I know and trust? How would I respond knowing it was God, whom I do not actually know? How do I trust that what I am doing is good, right, and appropriate? How will others understand that what I am doing is connected with God?

The answer Jesus would have given is, God is in charge. God is always, ultimately, in charge.

Bread Of The Presence

Consider Jesus' use of bread here and his choice of bread as an element of Communion. Both nourish and give life.

Pharisees

During the Exile, the Israelites were deprived of the temple and escaped with only the Book of the Law. In their dream of restoration, they made the Law the center of Jewish religion. The

Law offered a pattern for Jewish life and became the soul of Judaism. Pharisaism grew from a focus on the Law and its interpretation. Pharisees and scribes were a group of lay lawyers. Sadducees were priests. Ongoing conflict between the Pharisees and scribes and the other power group, the Sadducees, brought tension between emphasis on a lay-interpreted Torah and the temple.

The Pharisees were strict legalists and were an exclusive, separatist group. Their precision and rigidity in interpreting the Law brought the development of the elaborate legal tradition. The Pharisees did not focus on politics unless it affected their religious life. Pharisees were the liberal democrats of the day while Sadducees stood for the old ways. Pharisees believed themselves to be the true, pious Israel. They expected the time when a descendant of David, the Messiah, would restore the kingdom on earth.

Sabbath

Paying attention to sabbath has a long history in the Middle East region. Sabbath first comes from a verb meaning to stop or refrain from doing something. Only later does it also mean to rest and be inactive. At first and before the first day of the week became sabbath, doing work on the seventh day was considered unlucky. The number seven and its multiples were important and in some ways connected with evil spirits. Several days of the month were regarded as evil days.

The observance of sabbath, moving from a negative to a positive practice, started with avoiding agricultural labor on the seventh day. Then sabbath observers stopped occupational work of all types and eventually followed the day with no work of any kind. In the Jewish tradition, early Jewish Christians, gentile Christians, shifted sabbath to the first day of the week.

Consider the motif of God's creating light on the first day and our re-creating or taking care of this holy vessel created by God on sabbath. Think about our focus this day of bringing light into the world of our relationships. Consider Jesus bringing light into the lives of those he healed on sabbath and enlightening us about God.

Israel gradually transformed sabbath into a day of gladness and a sacred day in honor of God. Keeping the day holy emphasized the relation between the people and God. As this positive focus grew, the Jewish idea of assemblage developed. People gathered at the sanctuary to worship God.

Despite ever increasing restrictions, the day was to be joyous. The original motive of the Pharisees was to protect the Law, but the Pharisees ended up being rigid. Sabbath again took on a negative focus with the buildup of rules. Acute illness or threat of human life brought some exceptions to abstaining from sabbath work. However, punishment for the violation of sabbath was extreme and could result in death.

Today, ironically, we work harder on our sabbath because often it is the only day we have to get things done. Consider using the time of sabbath so we can do the laundry, repair the faucet, and so forth. Think about the notion of building short sabbaths of rest, meditation and recreation into each day or five minutes of each hour. Consider the full meaning of sabbath when we begin summer months of worship.

What is the measure of ease, relaxation, and pleasure in today's sabbath? What about the "how" of our sabbath? Does present-day sabbath call for redefinition? Is there time for everything on the sabbath — catch up, rest, worship? How can we honor the holy and the sense of personal/relational wholeness on the sabbath, the interior life and the exterior?

Withered (Hand)

Many of the 54 biblical references refer to the withering of a plant, its fruits, or a tree. Withering is a metaphor for death, fading, cutting off, or not lasting because of some internal drying up of the roots (see Job 18:16) or external condition. The Psalmist uses the plant simile for the withering of the heart or spirit. (See Psalm 102.)

Might Jesus have sought out the man with the withered hand because he wanted to turn around or reinterpret earlier scripture? How might he have responded to the following punishment for forgetting God: "If I forget you, O Jerusalem, let my right hand

81

wither" (Psalm 137:5) or 1 Kings 13:4 or Isaiah 40:7 or 24? Jesus himself caused a fig tree to wither (Matthew 21:19). If the breath of God can cause grass or people to wither, when does God choose also to cause the breath to restore?

5. Gospel Parallels

Pharisees
Rather than name the Pharisees first, Matthew and Mark say only that *some* people were in the synagogue who wanted to accuse Jesus of doing wrong. (See Matthew 12:10 and Mark 3:2.) Luke calls them Pharisees early (Luke 6:7).

In Luke, the Pharisees address Jesus directly in the grainfield, "Why are *you* doing what is not lawful on the sabbath?" (6:2). The other synoptics are less pointed: "*your disciples* are doing" (Matthew 12:2) and "why are *they* doing" (Mark 2:24). In Matthew, "they" bait Jesus with the sabbath question. Jesus then answers them. In Matthew and Mark, Jesus addresses the Pharisees with the sabbath question.

Luke says Jesus knew the thoughts of his accusers (Luke 6:8). Only Luke specifies that Jesus went into the synagogue and taught (Luke 6:6). Only Mark mentions Jesus' angry and sorry feelings toward the Pharisees (Mark 3:5). Luke does not say anything about his feelings but mentions that Jesus looks around at them all (Luke 6:10).

Disciples' Hunger
Earlier, Matthew explains directly that the disciples were hungry and began to pick the heads of wheat and eat the grain (Matthew 12:1). Mark 2:26 and Luke 6:7 only imply their hunger.

Sabbath And The Law
Jesus tells the Old Testament story about David and his hungry men eating the priests' bread. Unlike Matthew, Luke and Mark emphasize that David *gave* the bread to those who were with him. (See Luke 6:4 and Mark 2:26.)

The priests in the temple actually broke sabbath law every sabbath because they ate the bread. Yet, they were not guilty. The crux of using the Old Testament story lay in these words: "There is something here, I tell you, greater than the Temple" (Matthew 12:6). Matthew 23:23 emphasizes the point Jesus wants to make about the Law, that the Pharisees neglect the important teachings of the Law.

Only Luke distances the sabbath and healing stories by saying that Jesus went into the synagogue on another sabbath (Luke 6:6). The following references clarify further the passage about healing and the sabbath. "Which does the Lord prefer: obedience or offerings and sacrifices? It is better to obey him than to sacrifice the best sheep to him" (1 Samuel 15:22) and "I want your constant love, not your animal sacrifices. I would rather have my people know me than have them burn offerings to me" (Hosea 6:6). Like Luke, Matthew says, "For the Son of Man is Lord of the Sabbath" (Matthew 12:8). Mark adds, "even of the Sabbath" (Mark 2:28).

Saving The Animal

When Matthew relates the story of the man with the withered hand, Jesus tells another story of saving the sheep that falls into the hole. He compares the worth of a sheep with that of a person (Matthew 12:9-14). Luke has Jesus refer to the animal saved as an ass or an ox (Luke 6:5).

Healing The Hand

In both Mark and Luke, Jesus appears to make an example of the man with the withered hand. He does not heal him quietly in a corner but brings him to the front (Mark 3:3 and Luke 6:8). Matthew adds that the man's hand became well again just like the other hand (Matthew 12:13). Luke and Mark say his hand is restored (Luke 6:10 and Mark 3:3).

Miracle 6

Stilling The Storm

Mark 4:35-41 (Luke 8:22-25; Matthew 8:18-27)

---

1. Text

> On that day, when evening had come, he said to them, "Let us go across to the other side."[35] And leaving the crowd behind, they took him with them in the boat, just as he was. Other boats were with him.[36] A great windstorm arose, and the waves beat into the boat, so that the boat was already being swamped.[37] But he was in the stern, asleep on the cushion; and they woke him up and said to him, "Teacher, do you not care that we are perishing?"[38] He woke up and rebuked the wind, and said to the sea, "Peace! Be still!" Then the wind ceased, and there was a dead calm.[39] He said to them, "Why are you afraid? Have you still no faith?"[40] And they were filled with great awe and said to one another, "Who then is this, that even the wind and the sea obey him?"[41]

2. What's Happening?

First Point Of Action
In the evening, Jesus wants to leave the crowds and cross to the other side of the lake. The disciples take Jesus in the boat. Several boats accompany them.

Second Point Of Action
A storm rises and swamps the boat. Jesus sleeps through it all until the frightened disciples wake him.

Third Point Of Action
Jesus speaks to the wind and to the sea. The storm stops. Jesus speaks to the disciples.

Fourth Point Of Action
The disciples respond with awe and wonder.

3. Connecting Points — Conversations

Interviewing A Witness From Shore
Asker: What did you see from shore?

Witness: Well, you know how the wind blows at the transition from day to night? And you know how just at dusk the lake becomes choppy? How then everything — the water, the air, the bird's song — seems suspended? The silence, the peace? Well, that is the calm I experienced. Only it was not the usual sense of night coming on. It was the abrupt suspension, midstream, of a windstorm. The wind did not just blow itself out. It cut off, wind, waves, everything — sudden stillness.

Interviewing A Disciple In The Boat
Asker: What about Jesus' asking you to cross the lake?

Disciple: Jesus is not a complainer. We must look out for him. Once people recognize him, those who need him often mob him. By nightfall, he is fairly well exhausted. I often wonder if his readiness to cross to the other side of the lake is the closest Jesus comes to saying he has had enough for the day. It is his way of saying, "Get me out of here, fellas."

Asker: Scripture says you took Jesus in the boat just as he was.

Disciple: You might interpret the words "just as he was" in a couple ways. One meaning is on the spur of the moment without any special gear or preparation beforehand. One might also say this is a story about God's acceptance of human weakness, God's acceptance of us just as we are.

Asker: This story reminds me of David's bravery as he went to fight Goliath. Saul told David that he would not be able to go against Goliath because he was just a boy. He trusted that the God who saved him from the paw of the lion and the paw of the bear would also save him from the hand of Goliath. (See this Old Testament pericope, 1 Samuel 17:32ff, for Proper 7.)

Disciple: Every one of us is vulnerable. Even so, God meets us where we are and offers strength. We disciples see Jesus as our protector. We also protect him when he tires. Sharp as he was with us, Jesus did quiet the storm.

Asker: This was not make-believe or exaggeration of reality. You were in danger on those waves. What about your waking Jesus and saying, "Teacher, don't you care that we are perishing?"

Disciple: I look back now and wonder at my self-protecting words. Here we were Jesus' protectors, and we had to call on him to save us. You must remember that we were raised on the sea. We know the patterns and rhythms of the day. Waves do not easily intimidate us. Storms rise unannounced. Nevertheless, even for seasoned fishers, terror can turn everything around. Fear sometimes expresses itself with angry words.

I still cannot believe that Jesus slept through the storm. He was exhausted. I do not know how long I struggled with the boat and the waves while Jesus slept. He had to rest. I kept shouting inside myself, "Do something, Jesus! Something!" He slept on.

Jesus could not help people from dawn to dusk if he had no rest. We were all going to die by these waves. We'd never see the shore again. We needed help to get to the other side. I kept thinking the storm would subside. Finally, I just blurted out, "Don't you care?" Of course Jesus cares. He cares about us disciples. We are close.

My words sound selfish now. Had I called up the words of the Psalmist during the worst of the storm, perhaps I could have overcome my fear: "The Lord is a stronghold . . . in times of trouble. And those who know your name put their trust in you, for you, O Lord, have not forsaken those who seek you." (See Proper 7, Cycle B: Psalm 9:9,10.)

Asker: Where does fear come from? I would think you disciples, of all people, would be closest to Jesus. Why did you let fear get hold of you?

Disciple: As a disciple, I am not immune to crying out in fear. I am human. Sometimes I am afraid and feel helpless. As a disciple, I have no special privileges that exempt me from getting into situations where I feel vulnerable. In your modern-day churches, do not outsiders sometimes say to members, "Your faith should protect you from trouble"? My association with Jesus is no more an insurance policy or a buffer from harm than is your church attendance. Sometimes, I even think my association with Jesus makes matters worse.

Asker: How is that?

Disciple: Because of being around Jesus, I am more aware. I see the problems around me more clearly. I see the huge gap between the reality of what is and the ideal of what should be. I see how physically exhausted Jesus himself gets from doing the work God has called him to do. You call me a disciple. Discipleship holds a variety of meanings: a believer, one who follows the teachings of a certain religion, one who spreads these beliefs. For me, more than anything else, being a disciple of Jesus has meant constantly learning. Following Jesus around all day humbles one. I sometimes want to go far out to sea to escape the responsibilities to which my commitment to him calls me.

Asker: Then why do you continue to be a disciple? What are the benefits of following Jesus? Is your faith as empty as you felt it to be when terror overcame you in the boat?

Disciple: Despite the fear that occasionally overtakes me, or possibly because of the presence of fear, I am coming to know another presence. With faith, I can ride out the chaos. I can call out and know that God is here. Having faith requires an active choice to withstand fear. Being faithful to that choice is what discipleship is all about.

I do not think a disciple is ever a finished person. It is like the confirmands in your churches. When they finish confirmation and make the choice to become church members, they are not ending or completing their learning. It is easy to have faith in theory. Confirmands are just beginning to ask the important questions. It is then their faith truly begins to grow. They must not feel our dismissal now that they have come through the rite of passage. We must offer them the support and encouragement that accompany being within the fold.

Asker: Let us return to this story for one final question. What did you mean later at the end when you asked, "Who then is this, that even the wind and the sea obey him?"

Disciple: Usually a boat-swamping storm has to circle a few times to blow itself out. This storm quieted as suddenly as it arose. It is one thing for Jesus to work healing miracles. You never know exactly the cause of the malady. Even I can explain away some healing miracles when I do not choose simply to have faith. I do not intend by that comment to downplay the healing miracles. Jesus' power to transform the world astounds me. It extends to the natural world, to the natural order of things, to the sea and the wind.

We fishers respect the sea and the wind. The sea and the wind hold considerably more power than a person in a boat buffeted by waves. Yet Jesus commanded the natural world to quiet down. It did.

As we have walked with Jesus and heard his words, we have also questioned his identity. Now I know that Jesus called us to be his followers. However, a disciple is also, maybe at first, more of a companion. Belief is not always immediate, especially miracles we see with our own eyes that seem to defy the laws of nature. I wonder if that storm was to remind us of the meaning of our discipleship or to hint of the future? Jesus' challenging my faith was as jolting as a smashing wave. I must tell you, when the wind and the sea became calm that night, I began to shake with both relief and belief.

Interviewing Jesus
Asker: Jesus, you quieted the storm with these words, "Peace! Be still!" Might you have gone on to complete the Psalmist's words, "Be still, and know that I am God" (Psalm 46:10)?

89

Jesus: Yes, however, another verse comes to my mind: "Be still before the Lord, and wait patiently for him; do not fret over those who prosper in their way, over those who carry out evil devices" (Psalm 37:7). Having faith does not mean not being afraid but rather meeting that fear with faith. To reach the other side of the lake in the storms of life requires partnership with God. Partnership flows in two directions. In our noise, we forget God's presence. God is with us always, but we must quiet our chaos long enough to listen. We must become aware of God.

Asker: When people were in distress and cried out to God, the Psalmist said, "He made the storm be still, and the waves of the sea were hushed" (Psalm 107:29). Were you also fulfilling that scripture?
Jesus: Your word choice "fulfill," is important. Many find me only to be a revolutionary. I come to make the word real, to bring the peace of God, and to enable others to know God as present and active in their lives. I come to fulfill the words of the Psalmist and other writers.

Asker: Jesus, there was an edge to your voice, almost impatient sarcasm, when you said to the disciples, "Why are you afraid? Have you still no faith?"
Jesus: Sometimes the people who are closest to us, those in our families or under our employ, miss the obvious. Sometimes the people closest to us are the most cynical and unbelieving. Sometimes it is with them that we lose our patience. If we cannot listen to those closest to us, we are nothing. I imagine my impatience with the disciples that night parallels that of ministers working closely with church boards and church councils. Their focus is on the work of the church. They forget or reduce human measures, or they become impatient with the individual needs of these serving people.

Asker: Jesus, what does this miracle tell us about God?
Jesus: Some ask, "Where is God in the chaos?" God does not desert us when waves threaten to swamp the boat or when the pressure of

responsibilities pitches us nearly overboard. God might not be obvious in the chaos; however, as our trust that God is with us grows, we find God present with us in the chaos.

Part of the wildness is our own rocking of the boat. God enters the turmoil as the still voice encouraging us to quiet down. God is a stable, calming force within a world filled with instability. We must approach God, that is, catch the attention of God so God knows we acknowledge that we are in trouble. When God becomes aware of our need, God sustains us. God expects us to have faith because God is in charge.

While this miracle story may not appear to fit into the pattern of the healing miracles, it is about healing. It offers healing for the soul. In your time, the spirit of your people starves. Acknowledgment of and caring for the souls of people is absent. This has resulted in drying up of the spirit. This sense of emptiness flattens the spirit of people like the centrifugal force that pushes players against the wall of a carnival ride. When we feed the souls of our people, they become buoyant with new life. They stay afloat. Waves too great for them to meet do not overcome them.

4. Words

Stormy Weather

The people of Palestine believed geography, climate, and society all interact; God made them all and God planned for them all. In Palestine, winter is the season of rain and stormy weather. November becomes an intense rain time. Drought is common with sometimes only half the normal average rainfall. Unlike Jerusalem in southern Judea where average annual rainfall is 26 inches, an average of 47 inches falls in upper Galilee. The rainy season alternates with bright sun rather than offering a continuous downpour. Transitional seasonal periods of spring or autumn are absent.

Meteorological terminology of the Bible defines a tempest as a gale. Rain is seasonal rain with a heavy shower. A storm contains wind and rain sometimes accompanied by thunder and hail. Storms require people to take shelter.

Descriptive terms of the destructiveness of the wind's force include scorching wind, hot dry wind, and violent wind. South wind is gentle and brings heat. North wind brings rain. A surge southward of air brings heavy rains in March.

Peace

"Peace, be still." Is peace always active? Is it ever passive, waiting, simply accepting readiness? Those who trust in God have peace. Peace means much more than the stopping or absence of hostility between groups. Peace is a full word encompassing a calling of God's blessing of wholeness, good health, prosperity, and wishing all good for another, including one's salvation. Peace, Shalom, is a greeting or farewell among Jews.

Recently, on a cross-country flight, the author sat next to a man who ordered a kosher meal. We visited a little and, as we left the plane, I said the richest Jewish words I knew, "May shalom go with you." To my surprise, the traveler said, "Good luck to you, too."

Shalom is more than a mere salutation. I was surprised at first to hear the Jewish man reduce my non-Jewish shalom to a casual good luck. He had secularized my religious offering. Then I realized it was I who belittled good luck because the Old Testament God rules over the fortunes of people. The traveler had wished me well in the idiom of my own language.

Old Testament shalom heavily influences the New Testament meaning of peace. In the New Testament, peace carries a broader meaning within the context of Christian faith. Peace includes restoration of a right relationship with God. Peace comes from God, so it is the peace of God we offer to others.

After several conversations with a weekend house guest from India, I gained a beginner's sense of the multifaceted nature of the Hindu deity. Sunday, Deepak Mehta, attending his first Christian worship, and I sat together. As is the custom in our church, we pass the peace (from John 20:19). Offering my new friend my hand, I said, "May the peace of God be with you, Deepak." After a pause, Deepak answered with earnest, "And may the whole God be with you, Dee." This time I paused, then whispered, "The peace, Deepak, p-e-a-c-e."

After the service, we laughed together at the confusion of language. We still managed to convey to each other the depth of shalom spanning our faiths.

Another dimension of shalom is evident in the New Testament. Biblically unique to New Testament context, peace also means serenity or peace of mind. Modern-day cliches have weakened the latter term. To avoid suggesting only the relaxation of a troubled or anxious mind, we might appropriately rename peace of mind as peace of the soul or peace of heart. Again, it is God whom we trust to bring this peace.

Appropriately, it was Jesus who acted as mediator to remind the disciples of God's peace. The chaos of a storm is analogous to forgetting our relationship with God. Chaos of storm reminds us to be aware of God's presence and to call out to God.

Faith

From Jewish heritage, basic belief in God is trust in God's power. In the New Testament and for Jesus, faith has to do with our relationship with God. Everything Jesus said and did presupposed this oneness with God. His union with God was automatic and complete. Is that why he could not imagine his disciples doubting during a storm?

For Jesus, the starting point is trusting God as a parent who heals and helps us when we need. Absence of faith is alienation. God is present; we are the ones who separate ourselves from God. Being apart from God is a sinful condition.

Faith is our way of saying yes to God. Faith is belief in something or trust in some person or in God. It is a kind of knowledge without proof beforehand. Those who do not put faith first sink.

Disciple Who Called Out To Jesus

Whoever the disciple was who called out to Jesus, hearers of this story easily identify with him. He could have been any among the disciples. However, Peter usually acted or spoke for the group of disciples. Peter stood out among them. Peter's name is first in the inner circle of disciples (Peter, James, and John). Peter volunteered to come to Jesus on the water in another story. Even as a fearful, imperfect person, the fisher also may have taken the lead the night of the storm.

5. Gospel Parallels

Compared with Matthew and Luke, who used the common Q source, Mark is terse and to the point. The Gospel of Mark was written about a decade earlier than the other Synoptic Gospels. According to Pherigo (See *The Interpreter's One-Volume Commentary*), Mark was a contemporary of Paul. Mark, who was from a background of liberal, Hellenistic Judaism rather than the Judaism of Jerusalem, was probably a key member of the gentile Christian community and wrote from that perspective. He wrote about 35 years after the events he described.

The Setting
When? The Gospel called Mark says, "On that day, when evening had come" (Mark 4:35). Luke says, "One day" (Luke 8:22). Matthew does not tell us when the event happened.

Where? Mark (4:35) and Luke (8:22) also quote Jesus, "Let us go across to the other side." Luke, speaking to an audience as a storyteller from a greater distance, adds "of the lake."

Why? Mark suggests it was a spur-of-the-moment decision to get away from the crowd, because they took Jesus in the boat "just as he was" (Mark 4:36). Matthew presents Jesus as the man of action who "gave orders" (Matthew 8:18) to go over to the other side when he saw the great crowds. In Matthew, the disciples follow Jesus rather than taking care of him (Matthew 8:23). Of the three versions, only Mark explains further that other boats were with him (Mark 4:36).

Compared to the sense of urgency or tension in Mark's version, Luke's telling is casual on the surface. Note such terms as "One day," "a boat," and "So they put out" (Luke 8:22).

The Storm And Jesus Asleep
The Gospel called Luke tells first about Jesus falling asleep;

then he tells about the storm (Luke 8:23). Matthew and Mark describe the storm first. For all three writers, the storm is intense, with Matthew and Mark using the word "great" and the boat being "swamped" (Matthew 8:23 and Mark 4:37).

Luke and Matthew tell the story from a slight distance: "A windstorm swept down on the lake . . . and they were in danger" (Luke 8:23) and "a windstorm arose on the sea" (Matthew 8:24). Mark's telling is closest to the action. Mark's words are the most dramatic; for example, the waves "beat" into the boat (Mark 4:37). When Mark says a great windstorm arose, readers insert "right here."

Then Luke and Matthew add "but" Jesus was asleep, as if to say: Can you believe in the middle of all this Jesus was able to sleep? Mark says that Jesus was sleeping and details that he was in the stern, asleep on a cushion (Mark 4:38).

Response Of The Disciples
In all three narratives, "We are perishing" is the exclamation the disciples make in waking up Jesus (Matthew 8:25, Mark 4:38 and Luke 8:24). In Mark, they call him "teacher" (Mark 4:38), in Matthew the disciples call him "lord" (Matthew 8:25), and in Luke, they shout at him, "Master" (Luke 8:24).

Mark's words have a touch of irritation: "Do you not care that we are perishing?" (Mark 4:38). Matthew's words are to the point: "Save us. We are perishing" (Matthew 8:25).

After the quieting of the storm, Mark describes the disciples as filled with great awe (Mark 4:41). Luke says they are afraid and amazed (Luke 8:25). Matthew says they are amazed (Matthew 8:27).

Mark and Luke say the disciples speak to each other while Matthew uses the general, "saying" (Matthew 8:27). Both Mark and Luke say "Who then is this..." (Mark 4:41 and Luke 8:25). Luke makes Jesus the actor, that is, "he commands" (Luke 8:25). All three writers emphasize the obedience of the wind and the sea (Matthew 8:27, Mark 4:41, and Luke 8:25).

Response Of Jesus

The sequence in both Mark and Luke begins with Jesus waking up, rebuking the wind, and speaking to the sea (Mark 4:39 and Luke 8:24). Then Jesus addresses the disciples (Mark 4:39, 40 and Luke 8:24, 25).

However, in Matthew, before Jesus even gets up, he first responds to the disciples. He asks them why they are afraid (Matthew 8:26). Then he rises and rebukes the winds and the sea. Only Mark gives the words that Jesus says to the sea, "Peace! Be still!" (See Mark 4:39.)

In all three narratives, Jesus admonishes the disciples about their faith. In Luke 8:25, he says to them, "Where is your faith?" For a second time in the story, Mark lets irritation show in the exchange. He has Jesus say, "Have you *still* no faith" (Mark 4:40), whereas in Matthew Jesus addresses the disciples as "you of little faith" (Matthew 8:26).

Response Of The Storm

Matthew (8:26) and Mark (4:39) describe the result as "a dead calm." Luke says, "There was a calm" (8:24).

Proper 8, Pentecost 6, Ordinary Time 13

Miracle 7

Two Healings
The Daughter Of Jairus and The Hemorrhaging Woman

Mark 5:21-43 (Matthew 9:18-26; Luke 8:40-56)

---

1. Text

When Jesus had crossed again in the boat to the other side, a great crowd gathered around him; and he was by the sea.[21] Then one of the leaders of the synagogue named Jairus came and, when he saw him, fell at his feet[22] and begged him repeatedly, "My little daughter is at the point of death. Come and lay your hands on her, so that she may be made well, and live."[23] So he went with him. And a large crowd followed him and pressed in on him.[24]

Now there was a woman who had been suffering from hemorrhages for twelve years.[25] She had endured much under many physicians, and had spent all that she had; and she was no better, but rather grew worse.[26] She had heard about Jesus, and came up behind him in the crowd and touched his cloak,[27] for she said, "If I but touch his clothes, I will be made well."[28] Immediately her hemorrhage stopped; and she felt in her body that she was healed of her disease.[29] Immediately aware that power had gone forth from him, Jesus turned about in the crowd and said, "Who touched my clothes?"[30] And his disciples said to him, "You see the crowd pressing in on you; how can you say, 'Who touched me?'"[31] He looked all around to see who had done it.[32] But the woman, knowing what had happened to her, came in fear and trembling, fell down before him, and told him the whole truth.[33] He said to her, "Daughter, your faith has made you well; go in peace, and be healed of your disease."[34]

97

While he was still speaking, some people came from the leader's house to say, "Your daughter is dead. Why trouble the teacher any further?"[35] *But overhearing what they said, Jesus said to the leader of the synagogue, "Do not fear, only believe."*[36] *He allowed no one to follow him except Peter, James, and John, the brother of James.*[37] *When they came to the house of the leader of the synagogue, he saw a commotion, people weeping and wailing loudly.*[38] *When he had entered, he said to them, "Why do you make a commotion and weep? The child is not dead but sleeping."*[39] *And they laughed at him. Then he put them all outside, and took the child's father and mother and those who were with him, and went in where the child was.*[40] *He took her by the hand and said to her, "Talitha cum," which means, "Little girl, get up!"*[41] *And immediately the girl got up and began to walk about (she was twelve years of age). At this they were overcome with amazement.*[42] *He strictly ordered them that no one should know this, and told them to give her something to eat.*[43]

2. What's Happening?

By interjecting the story of the woman who suffered from hemorrhages into the middle of the story of Jairus' sick daughter, the writers suggest these two miracles are designed to be studied together.

First Point Of Action
As a crowd gathers around Jesus, who had just crossed the water, Jairus, a synagogue official, comes to Jesus and begs him to save his sick daughter. Jesus goes with him, the crowd following and pressing in on him as he goes.

Second Point Of Action
In the middle of this story, the Gospel called Mark interrupts with a second miracle story. As Jesus walks, a woman suffering from years of hemorrhaging touches his robe. Jesus, aware of power flowing from him, turns, asking who touched him. The woman comes forth to explain. Jesus speaks to her. His disciples say they

cannot see how he could possibly tell who touched him in this crowd.

Third Point Of Action

The writer picks up the thread of the first story with a messenger coming from Jairus' house saying it was too late for the child. The messenger does not tell Jesus directly, but Jesus overhears him and responds.

Fourth Point Of Action

Jesus goes to the house. When he tells onlookers the child is only sleeping, they laugh at him. Sending everyone away except the parents, he takes the child by the hand and tells her to get up. The parents are amazed. Jesus orders them to secrecy and tells them to feed their daughter.

3. Connecting Points — Conversations

Interviewing Jairus

Asker: Jairus, even though you were sure your daughter was dying, you begged Jesus to come to your home and lay his hands on her. What gave you the strength to endure this ordeal?

Jairus: Belief. I don't think believing is ever easy, particularly when things happen suddenly. My daughter was at the point of death. That throws a parent into chaos. Really believing is like staking your life on something when you very well might lose it. Believing is like bravery. Real bravery does not come from the innocence of the untried but from knowing the risks and doing something anyway. It is far more than an attitude of "I have nothing to lose so …."

When they came from my house saying my child had already died, I did not want to believe the messenger. Yet, I could not hide my fear. Jesus saw fear take over my face and heard it shake my voice. He spoke directly to my agony. He told me not to fear, only to believe. So that's what I did. That's all I concentrated on. Do not fear, only believe.

Asker: Despite what Jesus told you, when he took your daughter by the hand, you were amazed.

Jairus: Despite my choice to believe, I did not know if my child would live. I had to hope. Sometimes hope, the leap of faith, is all we have. Hope is hope. It is not certainty. I am human. Not everyone has the capacity to give trust completely to another. I am vulnerable to fear and to the facts of reality.

I was amazed because Jesus actually did heal my daughter. I was so amazed that Jesus had to call me back to the practical. When he gave my little girl back into my wife's and my hands, he had to remind me that my child was hungry, that I was in charge of her again. We had turned her over to God. Now it was our responsibility to care for her again and to give her nourishment. I realized from this that parents must be in partnership with God in raising their children. Even when we are most alone, God does not desert us. Ultimately, God is in charge.

Interviewing The Woman

Asker: When I read your story, I heard you crying this Psalm all those years of waiting and suffering:

> *Out of the depths I cry to you, O Lord. Lord, hear my voice! Let your ears be attentive to the voice of my supplications! I wait for the Lord, my soul waits, and in his word I hope; my soul waits for the Lord more than those who watch for the morning, more than those who watch for the morning. O Israel, hope in the Lord! For with the Lord there is steadfast love, and with him is great power to redeem.*
>
> (See Psalm 130, this week's lection.)

Twelve years is a long time to be suffering from hemorrhage both in terms of the physical drain and the exhaustion of your spirit. How have you endured?

Woman: Twelve years is a long time for depletion of the body, the purse, and the spirit. The cycle of hope and struggle has repeated itself many times in my life. In a way, my struggle has sharpened my focus on what is most important.

100

Over the long run, my urge to live as a whole person beyond malady has given me the energy and the courage to seek out many healers and physicians. It has been a journey up the wall of the well and back down into a pit. What I found strange in all this is the sustenance of hope.

The hope for a cure from one physician brings impetus to try again. Each time an anticipated cure hasn't worked, I have felt totally exhausted and wanted to give up. Always, in the back of my mind, I hoped that someday someone would know what to do.

Asker: You said if you could but touch Jesus' clothes, you would be made well. Where does your faith come from?
Woman: Prolonged illness has made me selfish.[1] My illness has pulled me back into myself. If someone has a nagging problem that just won't go away, the problem continually calls. Illness requires most of our attention. It depletes strength for life.

When I heard about Jesus' healing touch, I knew I would find him. The longer my search, the more I believed he could help. But his time was filled. I wondered if I would ever reach him. I came to believe, well, I guess it was like standing in line for something you must have for survival. There is no other alternative.

I feared becoming totally disillusioned before I would ever find Jesus. To my surprise, the opposite happened. The closer I came to Jesus, the more certain I was he could heal me. As it became obvious the crowd was keeping us separate simply because of the numbers, I abandoned speaking directly with him. I began reaching out just to touch him. Then, there he was. I touched his clothes.

Asker: What happened when you touched Jesus' clothing?
Woman: I knew from that moment my life changed. It's strange, this business of wanting to give up, of almost settling for less, for a compromise. But, you must understand, I am more than this illness. Something from deep inside kept me going, deepening my faith. Is that what a miracle is all about? I certainly couldn't be passive about approaching Jesus. Passivity is not my nature.

Maybe my initiative makes this miracle unique. I sought Jesus. I was stubborn enough to persist. I was doing the acting. I have heard that some other suffering people whom Jesus healed did not even call out to him. Either Jesus spotted them and initiated the healing or their friends interceded.

When Jesus asked who touched him, I knew the healing was real. If Jesus himself acknowledged power draining from him, then certainly I had not imagined it. I know well the feeling of energy draining, but this was not lost, wasted energy. This energy was spent to empower another's healing. It turned my life around from being depleted to being filled. At the same time, I was scared.

Asker: Scared?
Woman: Remember, I was ostracized. I was unclean because of the bleeding. Although the writer does not give me a name, I do stand out as woman. Only a woman can have my illness. I was forbidden to touch anything holy. I should not even have been there in the crowd. Any hemorrhaging woman is in a demeaning position.

Interviewing Jesus
Asker: Jesus, as usual, you do not waste words in these two miracles. You asked, "Who touched my clothes?" Then, you made little of the woman's touching. When you reached out to the child, you not only touched her but took her by the hand and drew her up. Don't you know, Jesus, what an unholy bind we have gotten ourselves into today with touching?
Jesus: First of all, it is precisely when one is most untouchable, such as the bleeding woman in my time, that we are called to reach out with the healing touch. It is precisely when one is most unloveable that we are called to love. A handclasp or the gentle meeting of eyes can be a welcome touch, an invitation to return to life.

Now, about unholy touch. Touch, human contact, is a connecting point between the tangible and the intangible. It symbolizes the faith that connects us with each other and to God.

I once told Jairus, "Do not fear, only believe." These words held one meaning in my early ministry. They hold even fuller connotations in your time when caution and distrust also threaten to violate relationships. Yours is an era when wrongful body contact must awaken caution. We also need to see that Christians are called to teach each other to become sensitive both to unholy touch and to holy touch. Might we call this spirit of gentleness educated trust? If we are to be Christian, at some point we must choose to let trust transcend fear.

Asker: Jesus, both persons you healed in these two miracles are female. One is the daughter of a high official. The other, an adult, essentially is ostracized from society because of her illness. You called the hemorrhaging woman "daughter," as if you claimed her in the same way Jairus claimed his daughter.
Jesus: I do claim her as family. As unacceptable as she must have felt all her adult life, she needed claiming. She needed to hear that she is accepted as part of God's family. All who stood around her that day also needed to hear this truth.

It might be argued that the writers juxtaposed these two stories to illustrate the socially accepted and socially unaccepted "daughters." I say everyone is acceptable. We must see the person first before we look at any of the superficial circumstances we tend to connect with that person's identity.

Asker: Jesus, when you healed the little child, you addressed her directly. Similarly, when you spoke to the hemorrhaging woman, you spoke face to face.
Jesus: Both participated actively in their healing. The bleeding woman sought me out. When I told the child to get up, something within her responded. She got up. Healing involves the whole person. Despite how it may look to the casual observer, God does not stand out there somewhere ready to tap us with a magic wand.

Asker: Jesus, what do you mean for these two miracles to tell us about God?
Jesus: First of all, God listens. God heard what Jairus said, then went with him to his house. God goes with us when we need help. God accepts what we say when we speak the truth. God believes our trust in our creator and sustainer. All this is obvious in the little

103

word "so." Jairus asked me to come and lay my hands on his daughter, so that she may be made well, and live. (See Mark 5:23.) So I went with Jairus to his home.

God notices even the least noticable and God persists. With the woman, I felt someone draw energy from me. Despite the chiding of my disciples, I needed to find that person for her sake. Despite the messenger's words and the ready mourners outside the house of Jairus, I needed to get to that little child just in case there was still something God could do for her.

God recognizes the role people play in getting well. Our task is to have faith. In giving the bleeding woman the blessing of the ancient Shalom words "Go in peace," God means well for us. I wonder if the words "be healed," are not also a recognition of the mystery and the miracle of the healing process. God did not say, "Here, I heal you." Neither in this instance did God say, "You healed yourself." Rather, God said, "Your faith made you well." Perhaps this is the key link between these two miracles: the father's "so" and the woman's persistence.

Further, God's focus is not on God. God heals because God cares for us and loves us. God is in charge. God is not easily swayed. By ignoring the nay-sayers, doubters, and even the realists, God teaches us how to manage the negative voices in our lives. Go ahead and believe, God says. By encouraging Jairus not to fear but to believe, God nudges us toward positive attitudes and a greater spiritual depth.

4. Words

Hemorrhage

Any bleeding, whether visible or concealed, great or small, was called hemorrhaging in the day of Jesus. Scholars suggest the woman's difficulty probably stemmed from a uterine fibroid.

Because blood was considered sacred, all contact with it was prohibited. In the Old Testament, bleeding was seen as a ceremonial defilement. According to the laws of uncleanness, a hemorrhaging individual was restricted in religious and social life.

The period of uncleanness for usual menstrual flow lasted seven days. Persistent discharge of blood from a woman required a considerably longer time of uncleanness. A person with a bodily discharge was ostracized because the priests believed uncleanliness was infectious, a sin, and the work of evil.

Touch

An unclean woman was excluded from touching holy things. According to current beliefs, when the woman touched Jesus' cloak, she would have been touching a holy thing and thereby making it unclean.

Today, touching itself has become suspect. Even the word "touch," has become tainted. Consider balancing negative touching with positive touching.

Jesus transformed the meaning of touch. For Jesus, touch was a means of communicating, a transmission of healing power, and a message that we are all connected. Touch is direct contact. Touch is spiritual as well as physical contact. Think about how touching relates to the leper or to a person living with AIDS. Consider that person, no matter what the circumstance, as holy, that is, touchable. When one is thought untouchable, consider the hungering for human contact — a hug, a pat on the arm, a meeting of the eyes that shows no disgust.

What about the phrases "rubbing shoulders with" or "shying away from" someone? What about not wanting to have anything to do with someone who is different? Think about the isolation, our projections of our own uneasy feelings, and our pre-judging. We sometimes avoid getting close to others emotionally as well as physically.

Daughter

In both stories, "daughter" is used. The little girl was identified as the daughter of Jairus, a synagogue leader. Later, when the messenger returned, he spoke of the child as the daughter. The child was defined by the father/daughter relationship. Although approaching the age of first menses and womanhood, the twelve-year-old was called "little girl." Although the hemorrhaging woman was probably of equal age to Jesus or older, Jesus addressed her as daughter.

Consider the following connections: (1) the prepubescent age of the girl child and the woman in relation to natural and unnatural biological changes, (2) purity and impurity, (3) the familial father/daughter relationship and the spiritual father/daughter relationship, and (4) the possible conclusion that Jesus was suggesting a guideline, that the spiritual relationship between God and woman or between mentor and follower is of father and daughter.

If one's own father/daughter relationship were positive, then one might think of these qualities: tenderness, kindliness, shelter, guidance, respect, encouragement. Consider these elements of a less than positive relationship: financial liability, paternalism, sexism, ownership, irresponsibility, absence.

Father is not a nasty word. One need not degrade the father in order to elevate the daughter's status. From the perspective of evolving mores in the year 2002, consider the differences between paternalism and fathering/parenting.

Jesus used the father/daughter terms as a metaphor for the positive, nurturing relationship he shared with his parent/God. Would we be more comfortable today using the inclusive terms of peer, companionship, mentor, and a sustaining, supportive relationship?

Talitha Cum

Of the three Gospel tellings of this story, only Mark uses these Aramaic words which translate as "Little girl, I say to you, arise." Aramaic is the language of common folk. It is homey and close to the heart. *Talitha cum* speaks to everyone's ears.

According to the *Interpreter's Dictionary Of The Bible*[2], three other connections associated with the Aramaic are worthy of comment: Retention of the Aramaic in a healing story emphasizes the aspect of healing. The Aramaic words lift up the miraculous event for gentile readers as well as show interest in retaining the actual words of Jesus.

Healing

Was Jesus ahead of his time as a healer? He understood the importance of relating to God as opposed to alienating oneself from God. Psychologist Robert Ornstein and physician David Sobel, medical school professors at the University of California in San

Francisco and at Stanford University respectively, and co-authors of *The Healing Brain*[3], suggest it is probably no accident that these words — whole, heal, health, hallow and holy — all stem from a common Indo-European root, *kailo.* (See *The American Heritage Dictionary.*) These words sing of a one-ness and an interconnection, a sense of the whole of all creation.

As we realize our bodies are holy because God created us, we honor both God and our whole being by trying to maintain the best possible level of health. Because God wishes well for us, we sense that healing is the natural direction toward mind/body/spirit wholeness. This circle of creation continues.

As a result, an attitude of eagerness burgeons. In one of this Sunday's pericopes, Paul speaks of it: "For if the eagerness is there, the gift is acceptable according to what one has — not according to what one does not have . . . . As it is written, 'The one who had much did not have too much, and the one who had little did not have too little' " (from 2 Corinthians 8:7-15).

Healing is more than only something external or done to us. Jesus understood that healing involves something internal to the person. Healing involves the whole person in partnership with the ingredients of the healing process.

When the physician in Victor Hugo's *Les Miserables* came to the house of Jean Valjean, he saw an old man whose will to live was gone. The physician knew nothing he might do could save the man's life. On the other hand, in her search for Jesus, the hemorrhaging woman brought her willingness to be well. The poem which follows touches upon these choices:

SOUL TALK[4]
*(An Imaginable Conversation With The Physician
In Victor Hugo's **Les Miserables**)*

*You speak of a mystery in your work
As a practitioner of medicine
Who learns to modulate science with art
When an old man says to you,
"I'm going to die" and you bow,*

There is nothing you can do
To turn around the man's will.

I speak the mystery of a woman
Whose body always has spurned the journey
Whose energy of soul finds
Another then one more way
In her work as a practicer of life,
And I yield, there is nothing I would do
To turn around her "I will live."

The body wants to heal. It wants to be as healthy as possible. When the internal healing mechanism of the brain can be triggered, the brain is quick and specific in dispensing its healing chemicals. This immediacy parallels the directness and quickness of healing in the miracle stories.

Who cares precisely how we start the internal healing mechanism as long as we can marshal up the forces for healing? One dynamic of healing is a partnership. Persons needing healing give themselves over to another power — to God or to medicines. By taking on an attitude of hope and by taking the best possible care of ourselves, we participate in healing.

Might belief or faith alone turn on the internal, healing pharmacy? Ornstein says we are "a sea of suggestion." Jesus' coming through the door at the home of Peter's mother-in-law, the arrival of the doctor, the recitation of a prayer or a healing ritual, the hope of the hemorrhaging woman simply to touch Jesus' robe, somehow distracting ourselves so we do not always pay attention to the chronic pain — all of the above could trigger profound emotional reactions with physiological effects.

What about positive expectations, faith, and the placebo effect? "Placebo," an inert substance used in control experiments, means "I shall please" in Latin. Does the cynic within us only associate the role faith plays in healing with cheapening, prepaid, healing exhibitionism? Wanting to give the credit to God rather than to himself, Jesus took care to separate his healing from crowd audiences and the embellishments of the enthusiastic. Still, the doubter within us at times prefers to diminish rather than to elevate the healing work of Jesus.

108

What if we were to redefine placebo as the will to please the brain's natural, or God-given, process of wanting to heal rather than as a physician's pacifier? The human brain carries an extensive role in healing. The brain has the capacity to influence physiological states. Studies of our decade show the brain's chemical neuro-transmitters, the body's intrinsic healing systems, may number in the hundreds. Among these natural, precise, brain-directed morphines are endorphins, dopamines, norephron, serotonin, and acetocolin.

Nevertheless, sometimes all the will and all the desire in the world to heal does not promote healing. Does that suggest a weakness of will? Ornstein concedes that management using the brain's positive influence works best in preventive medicine and in maintaining good health. However, eventually biological deterioration prevails. The laws of natural order still apply. Our bodies are still finite.

Even so, with a high degree of psychological hardiness, one is better equipped to believe in the capacity to improve or at least to hold negative and positive events in balance. Tell patients readying for surgery they have a fifty per cent chance of living and they call up hopes and plans for things yet to do. Tell them they have a fifty per cent chance of dying and they begin making funeral arrangements.

It still is possible to mobilize hope rather than despair. Despite having a less than perfect body, we can still maintain a sense of well-being. Healing, however, is more than willpower. The miracle of God's action in healing remains a mystery.

Faith

Some degree of faith is conditional to healing. Jesus presupposed divine love and faith on the part of either suffering persons or someone connected with them. For Jesus, healing was not only physical or psychological but also spiritual.

Healing is not somehow entirely our doing. We yearn to be totally in control of our bodies. Yet, when the body does not heal, it is not necessarily due to a weak faith. When the body cannot heal, it cannot heal despite the immune system and white blood cells usually given as part of human creation. Sometimes the body cannot heal because it has lasted as long as it can.

5. Gospel Parallels

All three Synoptic Gospels tell these two healing miracles, however Matthew offers a condensed version. Matthew begins the telling as a continuation of Jesus' healings.

The Lukan pair of miracles is somewhat shorter but close in rendition to the Markan story. Mark describes the details of the setting of the miracle, that is, Jesus' crossing the sea in the boat.

The Crowd
In Mark 5:21 and 24, adjectives "great" and "large" stress the size of the crowd. Luke emphasizes the relationship or response of the crowd to Jesus (Luke 8:40). They are waiting for him. They welcome him. For Luke, later in the story of the suffering woman, the witnessing crowd again is important as the woman "declared in the presence of all the people" (Luke 8:47).

In the story of Jairus' daughter, the crowd is generally disbelieving and has already begun the mourning ceremonies. They ridicule Jesus' words that the child is not dead but asleep (Matthew 9:24, Mark 5:39-40, and Luke 8:52-53). Jesus heals the child only after he has dismissed the crowd.

Prefacing Jesus' words to the crowd that the child is not dead, Matthew relates that Jesus told the crowd, "Go away" (Matthew 9:24). Mark's version is more of a suggestion: "Why do you make a commotion and weep?" (Mark 5:39) Luke's even gentler report has more feeling for the crowd when Jesus says, "Do not weep" (Luke 8:52).

In Luke, the representative from Jairus' house speaks more directly than in Mark. Both report that Jairus' daughter is dead. In Luke, he commands, "Do not trouble the teacher any longer" (Luke 8:49). In Mark, he suggests not troubling the teacher any further (Mark 5:35).

Mark reports Jesus' response as closer and in present tense: "But overhearing them, Jesus says . . . " (Mark 5:36), while Luke's report is slightly removed, perhaps secondhand: "When Jesus heard this, he replied..." (Luke 8:50).

Both writers quote Jesus, "Do not fear. Only believe, and" Luke adds, "she will be saved" (Luke 8:50).

Both Mark and Luke report that Jesus took with him into the house the parents and the disciples who accompanied him (Mark 5:40 and Luke 8:40). Still negative toward the crowd, Luke states that Jesus "did not allow to enter with him" any people except for the three disciples and the child's parents (Luke 8:51). Matthew's brief telling makes no mention of the parents or the disciples (Matthew 9:25).

Jairus
Both Luke and Mark name Jairus (Luke 8:41 and Mark 5:22). Matthew calls him a "leader of the synagogue" (Matthew 9:23).

---

1. For further discussion of selfishness and illness, see Susan Sontag's collection of stories depicting eight frail men and women coping with their lives, *I, Et-cetera* (New York: Doubleday, 1991).

2. George A. Buttrick, Ed., *The Interpreter's Dictionary Of The Bible* 4 Volumes (Nashville: Abingdon Press, 1962).

3. Robert Ornstein and David Sobel, *The Healing Brain* (California: The Institute for the Study of Human Knowledge, 1987).

4. Written by Brauninger with copyright held by the author.

Miracle 8

The Deaf-Mute

Mark 7:31-37 (Matthew 15:29-31)

---

1. Text

> *Then he returned from the region of Tyre, and went by way of Sidon towards the Sea of Galilee, in the region of the Decapolis.[31] They brought to him a deaf man who had an impediment in his speech; and they begged him to lay his hand on him.[32] He took him aside in private, away from the crowd, and put his fingers into his ears, and he spat and touched his tongue.[33] Then looking up to heaven, he sighed and said to him, "Ephphatha," that is, "Be opened."[34] And immediately his ears were opened, his tongue was released, and he spoke plainly.[35] Then Jesus ordered them to tell no one; but the more he ordered them, the more zealously they proclaimed it.[36] They were astounded beyond measure, saying, "He has done everything well; he even makes the deaf to hear and the mute to speak."[37]*

2. What's Happening?

First Point Of Action
Jesus travels into the region of Decapolis by the Sea of Galilee.

Second Point Of Action
They bring a deaf man with a speech impediment to Jesus and beg him to lay his hand on the man.

Third Point Of Action
Jesus takes the man aside privately, administers the ritual of healing, looks heavenward, pronounces the opening word, and the man is healed.

Fourth Point Of Action
Jesus orders them to tell no one.

Fifth Point Of Action
They continue to tell everyone.

3. Connecting Points — Conversations

Interviewing One Who Brought Jesus The Person With Hearing And Speaking Impairments
Asker: Why did you bring this person to Jesus? Was he a friend? A relative? Had you tried everything else before to heal him? Why did you feel this man counted enough that he was worth the effort?
Bringer: I know you live in a time where you can fly from one medical center to another. Your physicians can scan the Internet medical data base in search of answers. In my time, health was a divine gift and expected by the faithful in Israel. When disease occurred, the sufferer could only look to God for deliverance. Only the exceptional person consulted a physician. Even so, medical science was in its infancy then.

Never did Jesus support disease as a punishment sent by God. I cannot explain it, but Jesus understands the whole person. When Jesus knows someone is suffering, he does not need a battery of clinical tests or long questioning. He has the capacity to size up the situation immediately from the inside. He can restore health to the whole person — body, mind, and spirit. That is why I would bring any person — a friend, relative, total stranger — to this unusual person.

Asker: The story says you begged Jesus to lay his hand on the man. You did not just bring him and leave him there. You interceded for him. You spoke the words the man could not speak for himself. To beg Jesus means you are in earnest, you come to Jesus humbly. Yours was not a command but an entreaty.

Bringer: Sometimes the best we can do for a friend is to stand with her. Your modern term for this, I believe, is advocacy. When people cannot defend or speak for themselves, we must speak for them. We must be their voice. Some call it social support. I call it human compassion.

When the brain of a woman with Alzheimer's deteriorates, she has no past and no future. We must stand with her in her present. We must defend and recognize elements of joy in her present. When trouble fills children with too much silence for a child, we must help children give words to their secrets. Friends and advocates keep an ear open for appropriate times to speak for them. By choosing to relate to people in this way, I am more deeply involved with what is most important in the lives of those I meet.

You spoke of the manner in which I interceded for the person with hearing and speaking impairment. Commands do very little other than to ignore the essence of a personality. Commands speak to our mechanical dimensions rather than to the heart. If I am to be a mediator who draws two persons together, then I must speak to the heart of each. I knew about Jesus' healing work. I knew and trusted what must be done to heal the man. Jesus must touch him.

Asker: Jesus asked you to be quiet about this healing, but you could not do anything but talk about it. Why? Mark said you were astounded.

Bringer: "Astound" is too mild a word for the wonder and awe I felt as I witnessed the healing of my friend. It is one thing to hear about the miracle of healing. It is entirely different to observe it. One moment my friend suffers, in the next he is free of that suffering. How could I possibly be silent when I know of my friend's hopelessness as surely as I know of my inability to change his condition? All I want to do is say, "Look! Look! See what has happened."

Asker: You said that Jesus has done everything well, even making the deaf hear and the mute speak. That suggests you had doubts.

Bringer: No suffering person must withhold or be restrained from coming to Jesus for healing. In a way, I was echoing an old saying. Do you know it? "A good name is to be chosen rather than great riches, and favor is better than silver or gold. The rich and the poor have this in common: the Lord is the maker of them all" (Proverbs 22:1-2). Jesus illustrated this saying well. Jesus was not only a talker. He acted on his faith. This miracle helped build his reputation as a doer.

You said I doubted. It is not that I doubted. I had not considered the possibility of healing or changing something that appeared given from the start of a person's life. We think the present reality is forever. Does this healing suggest that even what appears as a permanent hindrance in our lives is only temporary?

Interviewing The Hearing/Speech Impaired Man
Asker: Until Jesus healed you, you played a completely passive, silent role in the event. Had you given up? Were you totally unable to communicate, even with the yearning of your eyes? Was it the yearning in your eyes that drew Jesus to you in the first place?
Sufferer: Maybe what appears to the observer as passive is a role of waiting. I wonder if something within us must be willing to be involved in healing if we are to heal or be open to receive healing. Was it a moving beyond the anger, the frustration and the grieving over my condition that let me become ready to heal? I gave up. I came to the reality that I could do nothing myself to change my circumstances. Did that make me ready to receive healing? Did Jesus speak to my whole person? Did he address what specifically caused my hearing and speaking impairments? What if that suffering part of me that Jesus confronted and commanded had refused to open?

Asker: How did you come to the attention of the others? Something about you must have impressed someone, somewhere, to intercede for you.
Sufferer: When we know another person well, subtle things talk beyond speaking or hearing. A listening of the heart, an observing of body posture or facial expression tells us a lot about someone. Compassion propels some people into action.

Asker: You must have been bursting to speak and to be understood. The opening of your ears was done to you. The releasing of your tongue happened to you. As soon as you were out of this silent, soundless prison, you acted. You spoke. You had something to say. I wonder what your first words were. Whatever they were, you spoke without an impediment. You were frank and candid.

Were you aware of the double meaning of your silence? Others kept what you said as private as Jesus' taking you away from the crowd to heal you privately. We can only imagine the words that burst from you: "And immediately his ears were opened, his tongue was released, and he spoke plainly."

Sufferer: I completely turned around. My ears opened. My tongue loosened. I always had asked the why's of my imprisonment. Now, I entertain this new mystery of my release. Could this be the meaning of the miracle of conversion — a complete turning around of one's life?

Interviewing Jesus

When Mark reports this miracle, he is terse and to the point. Jesus reminds us of the busy medical specialist who wastes neither her time nor that of her patient.

Asker: Jesus, why did you take this suffering person away from the crowd? You seemed to know just what to do, as a doctor who sizes up a malady immediately and administers the cure.

Jesus: God does not flaunt healing. God is not a showoff. My task here was to act for the sake of this suffering person. I took him away to heal him in private because I respect his privacy. I healed him privately so as not to draw attention to myself.

Nevertheless, my actions did not go unnoticed in this important geographical area of the Decapolis. Even the outcast and even the foreigner or different person among us is worthy of concern.

Asker: You healed with a combination of touch and words. Jesus, how do you trust the healing power entrusted to you? How can we trust the special abilities we have been given?

Jesus: God is not fake. I am no impostor. I would say to you the same words I spoke to the person with the hearing and speaking impairments. Ephphatha, that is, be opened to the gifts and possibilities God has given you. Gifts are given. Gifts are to be used. Trust them as entrusted to you, as empowerment.

This person was among the poorest of the poor because he could not express himself let alone support himself. God does not discriminate between the poor and the rich. God pleads for the cause of both. (Refer to the Old Testament lesson for this Sunday, Proverbs 22:1-2, 8-9, 22-23.) We must do similarly if our faith is to be alive and is to make a difference.

One after my time understands what I was about here. He reminds us that God has chosen the poor "to be rich in faith and to be heirs of the kingdom." The writer of the letter of James recognized that if, without showing partiality, we are to love our neighbors as ourselves then we must act and talk. (See James, Chapter 2, which is the epistle for Proper 18.)

It would not have done for me only to tell this person so impaired in hearing and speaking to have faith. I had to act and speak to help this person. James said it clearly, "So faith by itself, if it has no works, is dead" (James 2:17).

Asker: Jesus, you do not have time to respond to everything I ask. If I may, let me speak some things I have been pondering about the specific steps of this healing. All this ritual suggests that God is as systematic and painstaking in healing as God was in creating. For me, to follow a ritual means to have a plan or a design. I see five definite steps in your action.

First, you took this person aside, away from the crowd. When we are in need of healing and when we ourselves are to help someone, perhaps it is best to remove ourselves from the mainstream of activity so no distractions disturb us. Perhaps you are showing us here how to have complete focus and concentration on the present problem.

Second, you touched the person by placing your fingers in his ears. I could play with the meaning of specific formulae. Fingers in the ears might be your telling us to block out all other sounds of a hearing person to eliminate distractions. However, this man could not hear. Then there is the expression of putting one's finger on the problem. Another idiom suggests that God have a hand in this healing. A person is not just healed by another person.

More likely, you meant to remind us that human touch is as close as we can come to another. Yours was not a distant, hands-off approach. Touch is particularly important when one cannot hear you speak or tell to you something with speech. Your touch is the mark of compassion. This is a story about compassion.

I remember the story of the hemorrhaging woman. You said that you felt the healing energy flow from your fingers. Is that what happened this time? Is this method of healing to remind us to put our finger directly on the problem, to get at the source?

Third, you spat. Germs aside, beyond touching the man, you gave him some of your inner juice, a source of life-giving water. You are the water of life. You are the wellspring of life. Which is more important, the risk of more harm to the man or the chance of healing? This risk is like those of modern healing. We must balance the side effects and the potential benefits of chemotherapy and radiation therapy.

Fourth, you touched the person's tongue. Again, you touched. You made physical contact with the second source of his trouble. You chose to risk your own contamination.

Fifth, you spoke. You used words of invocation. What did you say to God, Jesus? What was your prayer? Your connection with God happened in a look up to heaven before you spoke, "Ephphatha." Is that method of connecting with God further evidence of your empathy with the suffering? You spoke in body language, common to you and the suffering man. You let him know that you were including God in this healing. Communication is far more than words alone. When we search for some kind of healing, we do not know what is going to happen, if perhaps we will come out worse rather than better.

What was your connecting with God, Jesus? You sighed. A sigh can be the action of letting go. Somehow, I think it was more than saying, "Okay, God, make it work now." Did your sigh say, "Not my will be done, Father, but yours"? Was it, "Now I turn his healing over to you, God"? Was it, "I've done all I know to do"?

As far as we know, you only spoke one word, "Ephphatha." The recording of this one word in the Gospel called Mark points to its importance. Mark did not say you commanded this to happen. I can imagine you looking the sufferer straight in the eye and quietly, but directly and with authority, saying, "Ephphatha." You knew what you were doing. You trusted God's intervention.

Asker: Finally, you must have told these people more than once to keep quiet about this. Why was this silence so important to you, not just in this healing but in other healings, too?
Jesus: Asker, you have given much thought to the specific steps of this healing. Before I go, let me respond to your final question. Some say I used reverse psychology. The more I suggested witnesses keep quiet, the more I meant for them to spread the word. Others say I feared misinterpretation or was exhausted and feared swarms of crowds as the word spread. Concentrate on being doers, not only hearers of God's word.

4. Words

Locale
"Then he returned from the region of Tyre, and went by way of Sidon towards the Sea of Galilee, in the region of the Decapolis" (Mark 7:31).

They called him Jesus, the Galilean. This was of broad significance for his whole career. Surrounded by foreign nations, Galilee was the circle of the Gentiles. Jesus would have reached a variety of people in his Galilean ministry. *Decapolis* encompassed ten communities south of the Sea of Galilee and extending eastward. Many travelers came from east and west. In later times, foreigners surrounded Jewish people. This was not always Jewish territory. This prosperous region was agricultural with wide diversification from fertile farms and vineyards to fig trees.

The *Sea of Galilee* lies straight north of and is joined to the Dead Sea by the Jordan River. *Galilee* was mostly north and west of the Sea of Galilee. There was an upper and lower Galilee with a rough central mountainous region. Lower Galilee comprised the fertile part of Palestine with gentle slopes covered with olive and fig trees.

At the north shore of the Sea of Galilee was Capernaum. Nazareth stood in the southwest corner of Galilee. It was near the border of Samaria to the south and the border of Phoenicia to the west. *Sidon* and *Tyre*, Phoenician towns northernmost on the eastern coast of the Mediterranean Sea, were considerably north and west of Capernaum.

"Ephphatha," that is, "Be opened"

Ephphatha is attributed to Jesus' healing of the man with hearing and speaking impairments. Depending on the version, "ephphatha" translates as "be open" or "be opened." The passive, to be opened, implies an opening beyond the control or initiation of the sufferer. The active, be open, suggests Jesus elicited the cooperation or the agreement of the suffering person. In some way, the sufferer played a role in the healing.

Did the impaired man recognize that he was or had become deaf and mute? We know only that someone cared enough about him to bring him to Jesus. Must something within us be willing to be actively involved in healing if we are to heal or be open to receive healing? Did Jesus speak to the whole person or specifically to what was causing the hearing and speaking impairments? What if that suffering part of the man that Jesus addressed and commanded had refused to open?

The opening is twofold: The man's ears are opened and the bond of his tongue is loosened. Jesus did not command the man to hear or to speak but to be open to these changes, to be open so that he might hear and speak.

What do our disabilities say metaphorically, symbolically, about us? How do they color who we are? What are those things that tie our tongues into knots? Are our ears to be opened to hear something in particular? To what do we close our ears? What do we not want to hear? What must we become ready to hear before we are to heal? What would Jesus or God have us hear?

Speech Impediment

If someone is mute, the impediment may be either voluntary or not at all by choice. Consider the bondage of a closed tongue. Have you known times when you could not find the words to express yourself? Have you ever been so conflicted that you could not hear what anyone else was saying, particularly or generally? Have you ever been in such turmoil that you could speak nothing with a clear mind?

If you had a lifetime, or even three months, of being unable to communicate, what would be the first words from your lips? To rest and heal her ailing vocal chords, Rhea Zakitch's physician prescribed three months of silence. Because of that silence, she said questions and queries of communication with her family took on new importance. It led to her creation of the communication skills tool UNGAME.[1]

Gayle Holtz said of her bright eight-year-old daughter, Nebraska's 1992 Cerebral Palsy Poster Child, "More than anything, I wish Katie could talk. There is someone inside there, a curious child wanting to communicate. I wish she could speak verbally with us because there has to be a lot she wants to say."[2]

While Katie cannot speak, she is learning to express herself by focusing onto a word board a laser beam from an apparatus she wears on her forehead.

Spat

Jesus' means of healing the man with hearing and speech impediments suggests a ritualistic formula that returns us to elaborate priestly cleansing rituals found in the book of Leviticus. Jesus placed his fingers in the man's ears, spat, and touched his tongue.

As part of this healing ritual, Jesus spat onto his hand, then touched the spittle to the suffering man's tongue, restoring his speech. Was this anointing a cosmetic technique with spittle of a symbolic nature and not strictly a therapeutic procedure?

This simple act holds a puzzle of meanings. One piece is the Old Testament superstition that believed human spittle contains the mysterious essence of the person herself. The act of spitting, a sign of strongest rejection and contempt, was as repulsive in Old

Testament times as it is today. (See Numbers 12:14 and Deuteronomy 25:9.) Figuratively or literally, to spit in someone's face is a disgrace.

Jesus gives new meaning to what potentially causes harm, the spread of more disease or injury. He makes the superstition reality by sharing of the essence of himself. Might one stretch metaphor, living water, to say he gives the energy of his life juice to cause the healing of another? Carefully and purposefully directing the saliva, Jesus uses it to heal.

What formulae do we concoct to free ourselves — a walk in the woods or by a stream or in the park? We make space for ourselves in the cocoon of our own houses or apartments. What rituals for freedom have you come up with?

5. Gospel Parallels

Setting

While both Matthew and Mark locate the geographical area of these healings, Mark 7:31 traces the specific route Jesus traveled, that is, "region of Tyre," "Sidon," towards the "Sea of Galilee," in the region of the "Decapolis." Mark's naming of the places reminds people living in the area who might become the gathering crowd that surrounded Jesus.

With the words, "left that place," Matthew links this healing miracle to the story of the mother and the healing of her daughter (Matthew 15:29). Matthew is more general, as if speaking to people who were familiar with the area, that is, "left that place," "along the Sea of Galilee," "up the mountain."

The Crowd

Beginning verse 30 with "Great crowds," Matthew emphasizes the number of people gathered to watch the healing event. Again, in verse 31, he refers to the response of the audience to the healing. The crowds are an active part of the entire story. It is they who bring those needing healing. They put the suffering folk at Jesus' feet (Matthew 15:30). They see the results of the healing. The crowds praise God (Matthew 15:31).

123

Although the crowd is secondary for Mark, Mark credits them for bringing the man with hearing and speaking impairments to Jesus. The crowd begs Jesus to touch him. However, for Mark, Jesus is the primary actor who takes the suffering away from the crowd to heal in private.

The Gospel called Matthew spells out the variety of sufferings of the people brought for healing. He relates their healing as a group. With half the number of verses, Matthew tells this story in summary fashion. Mark lifts up the healing of one person, the man who is hearing- and speaking-impaired. Mark describes the ritual of the healing. He focuses on the action of Jesus.

Crediting God with praise, the crowd, according to Matthew, connects Jesus and the healings with God (Matthew 15:31). In Mark, only Jesus does the connecting when he looks heavenward during the healing (Mark 7:34).

The crowd may have witnessed other healings. Mark's story suggests the crowd was observing its first healings by Jesus. Mark reports each detail of the healing. Crowd response focuses on Jesus and the unspoken dawning that Jesus is no usual person. Matthew reports no direct interaction between Jesus and the crowd. In Mark, Jesus orders the crowd repeatedly to keep still about the healing (Mark 7:36).

----

1. This resource is available through Cokesbury outlets.

2. From an article by Brauninger titled, "Creative Teachers, Technology, Family Have Katie Holtz 'Beaming' " in *West Point News* December 19, 1991.

Miracle 9

The Healing Of Bartimaeus

Mark 10:46-52
(Matthew 20:29-34; Luke 18:35-43; Matthew 9:27-31)

---

1. Text

> *They came to Jericho. As [Jesus] and his disciples and a large crowd were leaving Jericho, Bartimaeus, son of Timaeus, a blind beggar, was sitting by the roadside.[46] When he heard that it was Jesus of Nazareth, he began to shout out and say, "Jesus, Son of David, have mercy on me!"[47] Many sternly ordered him to be quiet, but he cried out even more loudly, "Son of David, have mercy on me!"[48] Jesus stood still and said, "Call him here." And they called the blind man, saying to him, "Take heart; get up, he is calling you."[49] So throwing off his cloak, he sprang up and came to Jesus.[50] Then Jesus said to him, "What do you want me to do for you?" The blind man said to him, "My teacher, let me see again."[51] Jesus said to him, "Go; your faith has made you well." Immediately he regained his sight and followed him on the way.[52]*

2. What's Happening?

First Point Of Action
Bartimaeus initiates the action by calling out to Jesus.

Second Point Of Action
Many around him sternly order him to be quiet.

Third Point Of Action
Bartimaeus persists.

Fourth Point Of Action
Jesus calls Bartimaeus to him and speaks to him. They talk and, regaining his sight, Bartimaeus follows Jesus on the way.

3. Connecting Points — Conversations

Interviewing Two Persons Who Were With Bartimaeus
Asker: You were part of the crowd following Jesus as he left Jericho. You must have been standing close to Bartimaeus because you told him to be quiet when he called out. Did you think he was not good enough to merit Jesus' time or Jesus' attention? Maybe you thought healing a person of blindness was beyond Jesus' scope. Tell us why you were stern with him and why you ordered him to be quiet.

First Onlooker: At the time, I was thinking more about Jesus than the blind. I thought the guy was making a nuisance of himself shouting out like that. However, when Jesus called for him, I saw that I was out of line. I thought Jesus was too important to bother him.

Asker: Did you not respect Bartimaeus as a person worthy of asking Jesus for help?

First Onlooker: Not really. You must be aware of how common the blind were in my day. They were always begging outside the city gate. They were poor. They were hungry. They were a noisy nuisance. Besides, God himself told Moses that anyone with an impediment of the eye was unclean and must stay away from the altar lest it become contaminated. You already know that uncleanliness and sin were the same in my day.

Asker: From what you say, people suffering from blindness were seen only as "the blind," the social eyesore of the day. You saw only the blindness and not the person.

First Onlooker: That's right. You start seeing everyone as a person and you start to care. I have to look out for myself and my own family.

Asker: Yet, once Jesus acknowledged Bartimaeus, you came to his aid. You said, "Take heart; get up, he is calling you."

First Onlooker: Not I. That fellow holding the blind guy's cloak is the one you want to talk to about compassion.

Asker: Excuse me, sir. Was it you who encouraged Bartimaeus after Jesus summoned him?

Second Onlooker: It was. Jesus caught my eye. He must have seen the look on my own face after they told Bartimaeus to be still. Jesus said directly to me, "Call him here." Now, Bartimaeus was no stranger to me. I know the family of Timaeus. I knew him by name when he could still see. In a year's time, he changed from a lighthearted, self-sufficient individual to an almsperson.

I kept thinking about all the flies and the blowing dust and glare in our region. Were I to be next to lose sight and livelihood, I would want to have the attitude of a Bartimaeus. When you are blind and someone does not hear you speak, it takes spunk to call out a second time. Suddenly, all the attention focuses on you. It would be easy, instead, to slip into the invisibility of one's own blindness.

Bartimaeus had considerable inner strength. He may have been blind, but he kept his ears open. He knew who was in town. He knew who Jesus is. I tell you, I took one look at Bartimaeus after they silenced him. His one hope to meet Jesus had been dashed. Do you know now how I felt?

Asker: I think so. When my daughter returned to Nebraska after a youth trip to New York City, she told me this story. She said, "Mom, I walked by all those homeless people in Grand Central Station. They were like things sitting there next to garbage cans, like moving human garbage. I did not even want to brush up against one of them in case I might catch something."

She shuddered, then continued, "Then I looked into the eyes of a young woman not much older than I. There was a person in there, Mom, a real human being. I will never forget her eyes. I could have been that young woman if our farm had gone under two years ago. I did not just want to toss her a quarter. I wanted to do something to get her out of there."

Asker: Why did you not cheer Bartimaeus when he first tried to get Jesus' attention? You did not nudge him to take heart then. Was it a matter of jumping on the bandwagon? Was it some fear of being connected with a loser that kept you from acting until Jesus responded?

Second Onlooker: You ask hard questions, my friend. Being an advocate for someone takes many forms. Sometimes we must have a collective voice to shout loudly enough for the suffering of a person to be heard. Look at the wonderful lesson your children receive in Dr. Seuss' *Horton Hears A Who*!

I was standing with Bartimaeus as Jesus passed by. I stood ready should he need me, but I would not further diminish Bartimaeus by taking over for him. Until Jesus was within earshot, I kept him informed of what I saw. It was up to him to call out to Jesus. He may have been blind, but he was still his own person.

Interviewing Bartimaeus

Asker: What about this, Bartimaeus? Why the loud voice?

Bartimaeus: When I could see, I knew how to judge distances visually. When I dare not miss someone, I sometimes err on the side of interrupting or being too loud. I knew the Son of David was near, but he was not within reach.

Asker: There is more to it than that. The second time you called out the same words even more loudly.

Bartimaeus: So you caught that! Have you never known desperation? I could not let him pass by without even knowing I was there trying. To dismiss someone is one thing. Being dismissed by someone does not feel very good. It made me feel blind and unseen by others or even acknowledged that I exist. One can either cower beneath dismissal or ignore it. I was willing to risk dismissal by

Jesus but not missing him. If I am going to speak out for myself, I am not going to whisper or mumble. People speak twice because they feel unheard or unacknowledged the first time. Persistence has to be a noisy nuisance to bring enough attention to effect change.

As for a double meaning, some say it was the demon within me showing itself as blindness who recognized Jesus as the Son of David. Demons in my day are the evil spirits, the bearers of disease. If even the demons within a person who is blind could see that Jesus is the Son of David, et cetera, et cetera. Well, I do not know about all those things. Most other people in my day believed blindness was sent as punishment by divine visitation. Like them, I believed that only God could cure my blindness. I believe that Jesus and the good Spirit connect. That is why Jesus had to hear me.

Asker: With blind people enduring such a history, no wonder it has taken so long for those with visual impairments to count in society.
Bartimaeus: Blindness is only the inability to see. I could still hear. I could still speak. I could still think. I could still act. Jesus acknowledged this, bless him, by addressing me, listening to me, and directing me to rise. Beyond this, when Jesus told me my faith had made me well, he spoke to the healing my soul needed. He went to the heart of the problem. For me, his power to heal is the freeing, liberating power of God that can overthrow evil.

Asker: Bartimaeus, in your short time as a person living with blindness —
Bartimaeus: Thank you for separating the disease or disability from my total identity. True, my blindness got in the way, but I am more than my blindness.

Asker: You anticipated my question.
Bartimaeus: Once people label or stereotype someone, they cage them in. They limit or ignore their potential. People in your day try to get beyond social welfare checks. I also refused to be the hopeless, helpless town beggar for one day more than I had to be. Let us make our own choice of attitude as we meet life accidents.[1]

Asker: Bartimaeus, I need to ask a sensitive question.
Bartimaeus: Ask.

Asker: As recently as forty years ago, people in my country did not understand some physical causes of blindness. When they could not immediately identify the physical causes, they tended to jump to conclusions. Bartimaeus, you shied from the demon talk.
Bartimaeus: I see where you are headed. Are you sure they only were not trying to study everything? I'll tell you what I think. When Jesus asked what he could do for me, I told him I wanted to see again. I think, as far as Jesus is concerned, questions about , to be crude, some craziness contributing to my blindness, some mental disorder .... To be sure, adjusting to blindness about drove me nuts at first. No, I think those are the wrong questions.

Look again at how Jesus treated me. Jesus received me as I was. Better yet, ask Jesus.

Interviewing Jesus
Jesus: Bartimaeus is correct. Although I used different methods of healing the sufferers of congenital and acquired blindness, I chose to heal both. Both types are valid forms of blindness. Sufferers may experience bodily symptoms because of mental conflict. They also may be in mental turmoil because of a clear somatic or physical condition. Ultimately that makes no more difference to me than whether a person was born with the condition or acquired it. All suffer. I want to reduce human suffering wherever possible.

You will remember from looking at the early miracles that I recognize that the condition of the various parts of the whole person influences the entire person. Therefore, I address the whole person. (See particularly Section Four in the second and seventh Cycle B miracles.)

Asker: Jesus, at first you were indirect when you instructed a third person to call Bartimaeus over to you. Did you hear him at all the first time? It took you time to hear what Bartimaeus was really saying. What finally stopped you? Was it really hearing him the second time he called to you? The urgency in his voice or the words he said? Were you testing him to be sure he was serious?

Jesus: Your words remind me of some time later when I asked Simon three times if he loved me. By the third time, he had pondered the matter fully. (See John 21:15-17.) The initiative we show in approaching God may be the turning point in healing. Please consider also that God may not always spot us at first.

Usually, crowds abound when I am involved in the healing ministry. It is a good time to draw people in. If I can illustrate a point, the people gathered will remember it.

When I spoke to a third person, the crowd around him immediately became involved. I could have asked any of them to reach out to Bartimaeus. As the brother or the son of them all, Bartimaeus became fully human and touchable despite the so-called uncleanliness of his malady.

Asker: You directed your next words to Bartimeaus, "What do you want me to do for you?" I expected you to say, "How may I help you?"

Jesus: The focus of my words was on Bartimaeus. My words offered him the dual confirmation that I heard him as one who counts and that he knows how he can best be healed. Like the Psalmist, he had taken the initiative so far by calling out to me. Bartimaeus' acknowledgment that I am the Son of David was ahead of the crowd. (See Psalm 34:4 and 6 from today's lectionary reading: "I sought the Lord, and he answered me, and delivered me from all my fears … This poor soul cried, and was heard by the Lord, and was saved from every trouble.")

Asker: "Go," you said. You sent him on his way. You sent him from you to be about his living as if to say, you do not need me, you can do it yourself.

Jesus: The actions of Bartimaeus in this story remind me of Job's showing God his faith. Job said, "I know that you can do all things, and that no purpose of yours can be thwarted." Consider also the following passages in today's Old Testament lesson as they relate to Jesus' conversation with Bartimeaus: "Hear, and I will speak; I will question you, and you declare to me" (Job 42:4). "I had heard of you by the hearing of the ear, but now my eye sees you" (Job

42:5). "The Lord blessed the latter days of Job more than his beginning" (Job 42:12).

Bartimaeus knows I will be with him always. I did not need to tell him to come, follow me. He already showed himself to be a follower.

4. Words

Blindness

When he asks to see again, Bartimaeus tells Jesus his is an acquired blindness. This result of eye disease or physical degeneration was frequent in Jesus' day. Climate, heredity, the aging process, and mental affliction contributed to the frequency of blindness. A severe form of conjunctivitis resulted in much of the acquired blindness. Flies transmitted the highly contagious disease. Environmental conditions worsened the situation.

Unlike the adventitious blindness of Bartimaeus, which happened by accident or chance, congenital blindness was also prevalent in ancient Palestine. Much blindness from birth, such as that of the man at Bethsaida (see Cycle A, Miracle 2, John 9:1-41), was thought to be the result of a venereal disease. No matter its source, blindness was a serious social problem because it brought poverty and hardship. Blindness also disqualified one from the priesthood. God told Moses to tell Aaron and all the people of Israel that no one with a blemish in the eyes or blind or with a list of other impediments could approach to offer the food of his God. Those with blemishes could eat the food but they could not approach the altar. The impaired were considered unclean and would therefore profane the sanctuary. (See Leviticus 21:16-24.)

Psychosomatic Origins

While somewhat hampered by psychological jargon, the following quotation helps clarify the role of physiologic symptoms in the origin of disease. The explanation is comparable to the approach Jesus took in his healing ministry. It is quoted from *Contemporary Psychiatry*, a textbook used in Clinical Pastoral Education:

> ... [T]he modern physician recognizes that emotions, en-
> docrines, external agents, trauma, and constitutional pre-
> disposition all are inexorably intertwined in the resultant
> physiologic alternations. What is neccesary in any event
> is to relieve the untoward stress so the body may regain
> equilibrium.[2]

It is well known that our bodies react to stress and that we all react in different ways to stress. In this textbook, Professor Snow says that extreme stress may come during early stages of life, when the human organism is limited in its ability to react to stress. However, the body of the organism is available to react biologically. When that stress is emotional, psychosomatic disease can result. The change within the organ is the same whether the disease is congenital or acquired. Only the origin differs.

Snow writes, "Whether emotional factors are primary and total or serve merely as one of the many stresses ultimately resulting in the creation of a disease entity, we regard the results as psychophysiologic."[3]

Any organ of the body can be marked for physiologic change in later years. At that time, the main help is to reduce stress and enable the body to meet the condition as best possible.

Could it be that Jesus had the unusual ability to recognize the possibility of emotional or spiritual origins of the diseases which hindered the sufferers he met? At the least, he knew what would help in each case. Perhaps that is the miracle. Another miracle, in our age, is that we are finally moving on from equating psychosomatic illness and imaginary pain. Jesus taught us that the idea of wellness is to remove guilt rather than add to it.

Cloak

When Bartimaeus sprang up to go to Jesus, he threw off his cloak. One can find both practical and symbolic reasons for this. One comes to Jesus unburdened by material no longer thought necessary. One comes as simply and unencumbered as possible. One comes naked, that is, without cover-up or hidden motive.

Teacher

Teacher is a title of respect and was a position of high honor in Jesus' time. A teacher is the counterpart of a disciple. The title held equal rank with a rabbi in the Jewish synagogue. To call Jesus a teacher gave him status as the leader of a group. It also recognized publicly the authority of his teaching. Both disciples and opponents of Jesus regarded him as a teacher. Because his work as a teacher was closely associated with healing power, the idea of a teacher was wider then than it is today.

Jericho

The compilers of Mark took care to place the setting of this story. Early in the telling, they referred twice to the city. Ancient Jericho was a major city at the southern end of the Jordan River. Herod the Great founded the new city. The New Testament city was a mile south of the Old Testament Jericho. On the west edge of the Jordan Plain, Jericho was the winter capital of the kingdom of Judea. Jesus would have eaten at the house of the rich Zacchaeus, who held an office in Jericho. Because the city was the scene of the temptations of Jesus, it also symbolizes the temptations. As Jesus left the city, he would have entered the main canyon on the way south and west to Jerusalem.

Son Of David

In the Old Testament story, God asked Jesse to show him all of his sons. One by one, God rejected them. He asked Jesse if he had any others. Jesse brought out another, his eighth and youngest son, David. God chose David. God said, "Rise and anoint him; for this is the one" (1 Samuel 16:12b). It had to be David, the chosen one.

Six of the nineteen biblical references containing the phrase "son of David" are from 2 Chronicles and Proverbs. Of these, five name Solomon, son of David, king of Israel. Note the lower case "son." The sixth refers to Jerimoth, son of David. (See 2 Chronicles 11:18.)

Five of the remaining thirteen references in the Gospels use the lower case "son." These verses include Matthew 1:1, which opens the Gospel as "an account of the genealogy of Jesus the Messiah, the son of David, the son of Abraham." When the angel tells Joseph about the conception of Jesus, Joseph is identified as "son of David" (Matthew 1:20). Given in the genealogy of Jesus in the Gospel called Luke, "son of David" follows "son of Nathan" and precedes "the son of Jesse" (Luke 3:31, 32). This tracing of the family concludes with ". . . son of Enos, son of Seth, son of Adam, son of God" (Luke 3:38). Jesus was not separate from the holy Old Testament line but part of the innermost circle. He was from the right family tree.

The Messiah inherits his dignity as a descendant of David. I have chosen you, Jesus. A name makes you special, Jesus. A name gives you identity, Jesus. A family muscles your actions and accomplishments, Jesus. The right name validates you, Jesus. Even Bartimaeus holds the identity of being someone's son. As sons and daughters, that is, children of God, we are all chosen. We all count, even Bartimaeus, son of Timaeus, whom Jesus chose to recognize and heal. Through Jesus, God claimed Bartimaeus.

After Jesus silenced the Sadducees when they asked him about the resurrection, the Pharisees challenged him. Jesus asked the Pharisees what they thought of the Messiah and whose son the Messiah was. They answered him, "The son of David" (Matthew 22:42). Again, in Mark 12:35, Jesus said, "How can the scribes say that the Messiah is the son of David?"

In the last eleven passages addressing Jesus as the Son of David, either the crowds or individuals crying for mercy give Jesus this name. Crowds of men, women, and children present at Jesus' healing of the man who was blind and mute (Matthew 12:23), add "Hosanna!" as Jesus enters the city on Palm Sunday. They call him "the one who comes in the name of the Lord" (Matthew 21:9). The chief priests and scribes repeat the name after his triumphant entry (Matthew 21:15).

In addition to Bartimaeus (Mark 10:47 and 10:48), among those who pleaded for mercy is a Canaanite woman with a sick daughter (Matthew 15:22). The remaining five times are in the three other healing stories of the blind (Matthew 9:27, 20:30, and 20:31, and Luke 18:38 and 18:39). This accounting reveals that even the lowliest and most needy persons recognized the stature of Jesus, whether they are pleading for mercy or praising him. From the long lineage of Boaz and Ruth to Obed to Jesse the father of David and again in Luke's genealogy, one might say, symbolically, that the family of God is large and all-encompassing. Jesus belongs to the generic family of humankind. The son of divinity is also the son of humanity, the link, and connector.

To be called the son of David has other possible meanings. With so many sons and grandsons in the huge family of David lineage, Jesus was another in the line. They might as well have called him the son of generic man as the son of David. Also this says he is one of us as well as belonging to his parent, God.

To call one daughter or son is to claim her or him as one's own. It gives the child a pedigree. Though possibly a child of mysterious birth, a child is legitimate because the child is claimed. Today the biological father does not always come forward and claim a child. However, as women claim their own names, their own authenticity, a single mother herself can give her child legitimacy.

5. Gospel Parallels

The Blind Person(s) And Begging

Of the four accounts of the healing of the blind person, only in Mark's account does he have a name. Mark clearly identifies him as Bartimaeus, son of Timaeus, and as a blind beggar who sits by the roadside (Mark 10:46). Beyond knowing his name, folk know to whom he belongs.

In the two Matthew parallels, 20:29-34 and 9:27-31, there are two unnamed blind men. In chapter 20, Matthew does not mention a beggar or begging. However, "they" are sitting by the roadside. They shout to Jesus when they hear Jesus is passing by (Matthew 20:30). In chapter 9, they follow Jesus as he passes by and cry loudly to him (Matthew 9:27).

In Luke's account one unnamed blind man sits by the roadside and begs (Luke 18:35-43). Luke says he asked others in the passing crowd what is happening. When he learns it is Jesus, he shouts to Jesus (Luke 18:38). Mark says when the blind man hears it is Jesus of Nazareth, he shouts (Mark 10:47).

Blind Person's (Persons') Words

All versions acknowledge Jesus as the "Son of David" and all ask for mercy. In all but the Matthew 9 account, the blind person(s) preface the request formula with Jesus or Lord: "Have mercy on us, Son of David!" (Matthew 9:27), "Jesus, Son of David, have mercy on me!" (Mark 10:47) and "Lord, have mercy on us, Son of David!" (Matthew 20:30 and 31). In the latter, the blind men twice shout the same words, "Have mercy on us, Lord, Son of David," before Jesus answers them. Luke records, "Jesus, Son of David, have mercy on me!" (Luke 18:38) and again, "Son of David, have mercy on me!" (verse 39).

Crowd Response

In Mark, many (from the crowd) sternly order the blind person to be quiet (Mark 10:48), which only encourages him to shout the words again. Also in Matthew 20, the crowd responds to the shouts of the blind men, sternly ordering them to be quiet (Matthew 20:31). This leads them to shout even more. Luke describes the crowd only as "those who were in the front sternly" (Luke 18:39). Matthew 9 says nothing about the crowd's response.

Jesus' Response

In Mark 10, Matthew 20, and Luke 18, first Jesus stands still. The Matthew 9 version differs at this point, with the blind men coming to Jesus when he enters the house. No middle person intercedes for the blind men. In Mark 10:49, someone in the crowd plays an active role. Jesus instructs that person to call the blind man to him. The crowd does so and further encourages him, "Take heart; get up, he is calling you." In Luke, Jesus also directs another person to bring the blind man to him (Luke 18:40). However, in the Matthew 20 telling, which focuses on Jesus as the main character, Jesus addresses the blind men directly.

In three narratives, Jesus asks the same question: "What do you want me to do for you?" (Mark 10:51, Matthew 20:32, Luke 18:41). However, in Matthew 9:28 the question is "Do you believe that I am able to do this?"

Response Of The Blind Person(s)

The men answer Jesus' question, "Do you believe?" with "Yes, Lord" (Matthew 9:28). Mark shows the blind man as ready, energetic and enthusiastic. He throws off his cloak. He springs up. He comes to Jesus (Mark 10:50). When Jesus questions him, the man addresses Jesus as "my teacher" and asks that Jesus let him see again (Mark 10:51).

The teller of Luke's narrative stands back from the action, reporting, "and when he came near ..." (Luke 18:40). The blind man addresses Jesus as Lord (Luke 18:41) as do the blind men in Matthew 20. In Luke he says, "let me see again" (Luke 18:41), while the blind persons in Matthew 20 ask that their eyes be opened, suggesting they have never seen.

The Healing

In Mark, Jesus does not touch the blind man but tells him his faith has made him well. Immediately he regains his sight and follows Jesus on the way (Mark 10:52). Focusing upon Jesus, Matthew 20:34 emphasizes Jesus' compassion in choosing to touch the eyes of the blind men. As in Mark, the writer stresses the immediacy of the result and that they follow Jesus. In Matthew 20, they regain their sight. In Matthew 9:29, Jesus touches their eyes and their eyes are opened. Note the passive voice. Then Jesus emphasizes the importance of their own faith in the healing.

The Closing

Luke's account is closer to Mark's but spells out the story more fully. In all the narratives, Jesus stands still in acknowledgment, orders the person(s) brought to him and asks the same question. The blind man this time glorifies God and the crowd joins in (Luke 18:43).

Only in the Matthew 9 telling does Jesus sternly order the blind men to tell no one, but of course they do (Matthew 9:30,31). Matthew 20:34 and Mark 10:52 both close with the healed man following Jesus.

---

1. For a fuller discussion about choosing one's attitude toward life accidents, see Gail Sheehy's book *Pathfinders*.

2. From Laurence H. Snow, M.D., *Contemporary Psychiatry* (Chicago: Year Book Medical Publishers, Inc., 1972), page 80. Snow was then Professor of Psychiatry at The Medical College of Pennsylvania.

3. See Snow, *Contemporary Psychiatry*, page 78.

Bibliography

Brunt, John C., *A Day For Healing: The Meaning Of Jesus' Sabbath Miracles* (Washington, D.C.: Review and Herald Publication Association, 1981)

Buttrick, George A., Ed., *The Interpreter's Dictionary Of The Bible* 4 Volumes (Nashville: Abingdon Press, 1962)

Hugo, Victor, *Les Miserables* (New York: Dodd, Mead and Co., 1984)

Jeremias, Joachim, *Jerusalem In The Time Of Jesus* (Philadelphia: Fortress Press, 1969)

Kee, Howard Clark, *The Origins Of Christianity* (Englewood Cliffs, N.J.: Prentice-Hall, 1973)

Kee, Howard Clark, *Understanding The New Testament*, 4th Edition (Englewood Cliffs, N.J.: Prentice-Hall, 1983)

Kee, Howard Clark, *Jesus In History: An Approach To The Study Of The Gospels* (New York: Harcourt, Brace and World, Inc., 1970)

Laymon, Charles M., Ed., *The Interpreter's One Volume Commentary on the Bible* (Nashville: Abingdon Press, 1971)

L'Engle, Madeleine, *A Circle Of Quiet* (Madeleine L'Engle Franklin, 1972)

Lewis, C. S., *Miracles: A Preliminary Study* (New York: Macmillan, 1978 edition, ©1960)

Metzger, Bruce M., *The New Testament: Its Background, Growth And Content* (Nashville: Abingdon Press, 1983)

Ornstein, Robert and David Sobel, M.D., *The Healing Brain* (California: The Institute for the Study of Human Knowledge, 1987)

Perrin, Norman, *Jesus And The Language Of The Kingdom: Symbol And Metaphor In New Testament Interpretation* (Philadelphia: Fortress Press, 1976)

Dr. Seuss, *Horton Hears A Who* (New York: Random House, 1954)

Sheehy, Gail, *Pathfinders* (New York: Bantam Books, 1981)

Snow, Laurence H., M.D., *Contemporary Psychiatry* (Chicago: Year Book Medical Publishers, Inc., 1972)

Sontag, Susan. *I, Etcetera* (New York: Doubleday, 1991)

Stambaugh, John E. *The New Testament In Its Social Environment* (Philadelphia: Westminster Press, 1986)